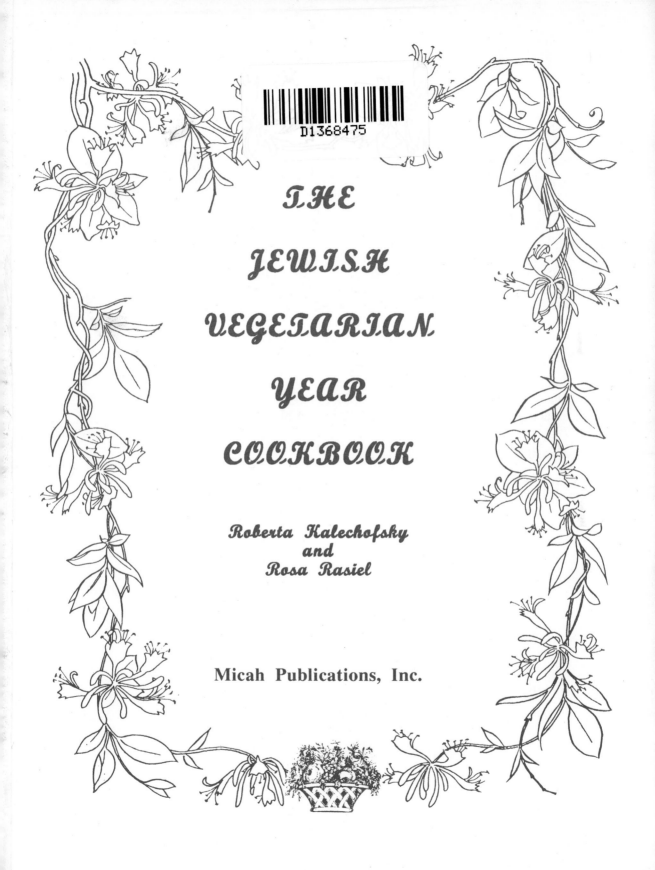

THE
JEWISH
VEGETARIAN
YEAR
COOKBOOK

Roberta Kalechofsky
and
Rosa Rasiel

Micah Publications, Inc.

The Jewish Vegetarian Year Cookbook, Copyright (c) Micah Publications, Inc., 1997.

Third Printing, 2,000

No part of this book purports to give medical advice nor is intended to be used for medical purposes, or as a replacement for professional medical attention.

Printed in the United States of America
Cover: "Fantasy On A Sukkah," by Sara Feldman
Production: Robert Kalechofsky and Roberta Kalechofsky

Other Illustrations: Jim Harter, *Food and Drink*, Dover, 1883; Carol Belanger Grafton, *Old-Fashioned Floral Borders,* Dover 1989; Carol Belanger Grafton, *Victorian Floral Illustrations,* Dover 1985; Charles Derriey, *Borders, Frames and Decorative Motifs,* Dover; Channukiah by Faith Gaber.
Special thanks to the Edensoy Company for their generosity in sending recipes and suggestions, and to The Jewish Vegetarian Society of Toronto for *A Haggadah For Tu Bi Shevat.*

Kalechofsky, Roberta.
        The Jewish vegetarian year cookbook / Roberta Kalechofsky & Rosa Rasiel.
        p. cm.
    Includes bibliographical references and index.
    ISBN 0-916288-43-9
    I. Rasiel, Rosa, 1935-   . II. Title.
TX837.K252 1997   96-44338
641.5'636'089924--dc20   CIP

Micah Publications, Inc.

Table of Contents

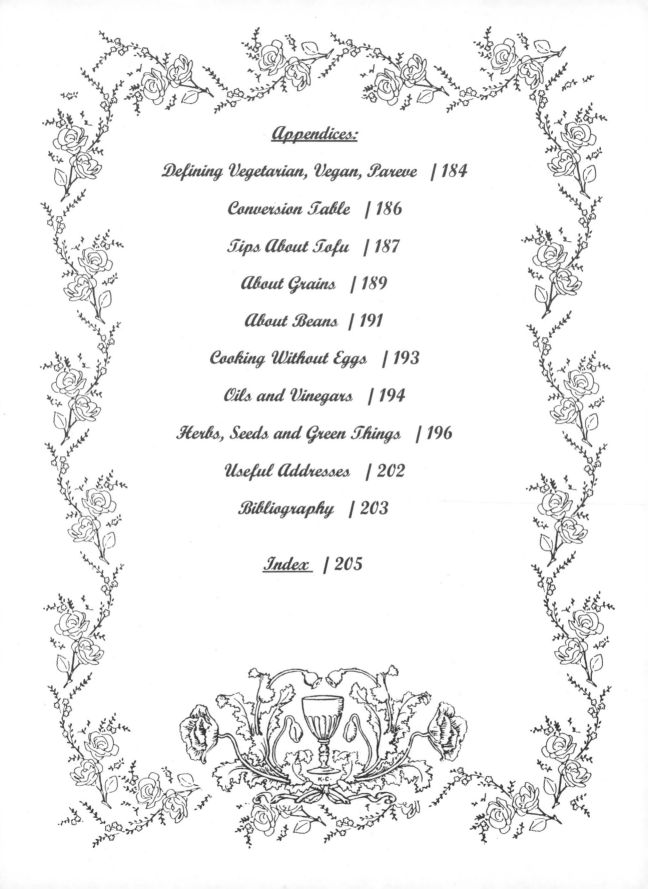

Acknowledgments and Appreciations

Few things are as pleasurable as the mixture of good food and good company. The making of this cookbook brought both together in a committee of friends who agreed to cook and test recipes. On a dozen or more Thursday nights, they came bearing gifts from their imagination and experience of soups, pastas, salads, and desserts. We sniffed, tasted, commented, corrected, and ate it all. The whole world should eat so well. To this end, we thank Laurie Hammer and her husband, Av, Madeline Shavelson, Irma Natan; Roberta's husband, Bob, who was voted "Prince of Tasters," a job he aspires to permanently; Lisa Rosenberg who tested recipes at home, and Naomi Rosenberg and Ami Rasiel for their encouragement and support.

Other people, as well as organizations, who were generous with recipes and with time in other ways were Evelyn Dorfman, a guiding spirit of The Jewish Vegetarians of Toronto, who contributed recipes and gave permission to reprint their Tu B'Shevat haggadah; Mimi Golfman-Clarke, an instructor in vegetarian cooking in Fairfax, Virginia; Gloria Bakst who took time out from her schedule as an instructor in Health Food Cooking and Catering, and as Demonstration Food Coordinator for Bread and Circus Whole Foods, to advise on recipes; Karen Davis, the founder of United Poultry Concerns, who taught us how to live without eggs; The Vegetarian Resource Group who permitted us to reprint recipes from their book, *The Lowfat Jewish Vegetarian Cookbook,* and the North American Vegetarian Society who were generous with recipes from Muriel Collura Golde's booklet, *Vegetarian Cooking For A Better World.* Their contributions, as well as those of others, are cited in context.

We are especially grateful to Sara Feldman, painter and illustrator of scenes across the United States and Israel, lover of fruits, vegetables and wildflowers done in the glow of summer sunlight. Her credits as an artist are manifold: they include seven one-woman shows and a multitude of group shows, editor and illustrator for *The Eternal Flame,* a 1983 prize-winning publication of Congregation Mishkan Tefila in Brookline, Massachusetts, as part of the Holocaust Memorial Program; designer of the stained-glass window in the Bacon Memorial Chapel of Northeastern University. She gave generously of her talent so that the cover of this cookbook, "Fantasy on A Sukkah," which incorporates the seven sacred species, would convey the joyous spirit of Jewish vegetarianism.

The Jewish Vegetarian Year Cookbook

Introduction:
A Short History of Kashrut and Its Vegetarian Implications

Our civilization is going through a period of confusion with respect to food, as we evaluate the technological revolution in farming, husbandry, and food processing methods that has overtaken food production in the last century; and as we try to understand the relationship between food and health. An article in *Self* magazine (Dec., 1995) pointed out that, "A poor diet combined with a sedentary lifestyle contributes to approximately 400,000 deaths a year-- the same as cigarette smoking--and yet the government's response does not go much beyond ineffectual public-service announcements and pamphlets.... As a result the public hasn't been persuaded that diet is crucial to its health.'"

The Jewish traditions of concern for health and for kashrut should prepare the Jewish people to grapple with this problem The Jewish concern for food, where it comes from and how it is prepared, is so well known, that for many people "kosher" is almost synonymous with "Jewish." The system of kashrut is one of the oldest and most documented relationships between a culture and its food, and has fascinated ethnologists and anthropologists for decades. The commandments, associated with holiness (Lev. 11:44-45], have conditioned Jews through millennia to know that the act of eating should be hallowed. For Jews, food is not only a nutritional matter, but a spiritual one.

Even Jews who choose not to live by the rules of kashrut have had their mental lives shaped by a heightened awareness of concepts such as "clean" or healthy food, taboo animals, and meat that is "fit" or "unfit" to eat; their characters and ethical concerns about animals have been molded by these influences. They share the feeling that what we put into our mouths constitutes a primary exchange between our interior selves and the outer world. Eating or ingesting is the earliest way we bring the outer world into our inner beings and "taste" reality. It is one of the first ways a baby comes to know the tangible world and to test its availability for his system. He finds something, picks it up, looks at it, tries to determine what it is--edible or not--a stone or a piece of bread---then pops it into his mouth to find out. We take in the outer world through our eyes, our ears, our sense of touch; but we ingest it only through the mouth.

Today, we are like the baby trying to define what is edible and not edible, what is healthy, fattening, carcinogenic, good or bad for our hearts, our cholesterol levels, our bones. Food for everyone has become more complicated than kashrut ever was, and kashrut has become concomitantly more complicated. The complexity of modern day kashrut reflects the complexity of our contemporary food problems. But kashrut was not meant to be this way. Adam and Eve had only two laws concerning food:

> *"Do not eat from the tree of the knowledge of good and evil,"* (Gen. 2:14)
> *and "To you I give every herb, seed and green thing.*
> *These shall be yours for food."* (Gen. 1:30)

In fact, they had only one law of kashrut: they could eat everything that came from the earth except the fruit from the tree of the knowledge of good and evil. Anything else that grew in the earth was naturally kosher. As long as they remained vegetarians, they observed kashrut.

But they broke the first law of kashrut, and Noah broke the second law after the flood, and kashrut has become increasingly complex ever since. When Noah set up a slaughter site and altar without orders from God to do so, the laws underwent their first complication. God gave Noah permission to eat meat, but with the moral price that humankind would know war and would be separated from the rest of the animal world (Gen 1X, 3). This permission was given with the restriction, applicable to the whole human race, that no one was to eat a limb torn from a living animal or consume its blood. We were not to take our meat as the predatory animals do in the chase, the hunt and the attack. The effect of this law (*"ever min hahai"* Gen. 1X, 4) upon Jewish character was enormous. It is the source of of the Jewish aversion to hunting which continues to this day. Jews had permission to eat meat, but not to be predators. Isaiah called this commandment "the ancient covenant" and regarded violations of it with intense aversion (Isaiah, 24: 4-12).

The next law of kashrut limited the meat Jews ate to those animals who were vegetarian animals. Not only were we not to take our meat as predators, but we were not to eat predatory animals. Under Mosaic law, meat for the Jewish people was hereafter limited to the "clean" animals or vegetarian ruminants, was separated out from hunting and became a function of the sacrificial system of a pastoral people. The animal to be eaten was to be chosen from the flock and sacrificed in recognition that its life belonged to God.

Some scholars argue that God attempted to make the Jews vegetarians during their sojourn in the desert. Manna was the symbol for this vegetarian diet. But there were two major threatening food riots, characterized by the demand for meat. From the very beginning of the revolution the Israelites were rebellious and Moses' position was often precarious, necessitating compromises with the eating of meat.

> *"The mixed multitude, [the riff-raff], that was among them,*
> *began to lust [for meat];*
> *and the Children of Israel also cried out,*
> *"Would that we had flesh to eat!"* (Num. 11:4)

There was a quarrel concerning meat, which is further expressed in Deuteronomy 12:20: "When the Lord enlarges your territory as He has promised, and you say, 'I shall eat meat,' for you have the urge to eat meat, you may eat meat if you wish." This, however, is not a commandment to eat meat, but a compromise with human lust. As Samuel Dresner points out, this permission is for meat of lust because it is not regarded as necessary or commanded food. (*The Jewish Dietary Laws* p. 25) Dresner calls this dispensation "a divine concession to human weakness and human need." Elijah Schochet also interprets the passage in Deuteronomy 12:20 as a grudging permission to eat meat.

"...is there a decree *demanding* of man that he butcher and consume the flesh of fauna? Should meat be part of his standard, normal diet? Not at all.
Quite the contrary. The crucial passage in Deuteronomy reads: 'When the Lord thy God shall enlarge thy border, as He hath promised thee, and thou shalt say: 'I will eat flesh,' because thy soul desireth to eat flesh; thou mayest eat flesh, after all the desire of thy soul.' Now rabbinic tradition perceives in this text a clear indication that it is man's desire to eat flesh, not God's decree that he is to do so, and attributes an unflattering connotation to this lust for flesh."   (*Animal Life in Jewish Tradition,* p. 50)

The general rabbinic judgment in the Talmud reflects an uneasy compromise. It acknowledges the human lust for meat and the occasional need for it. "Human consumption of meat," Dresner writes, "which means the taking of an animal's life, has constantly posed a religious problem to Judaism, even when it has accepted the necessity of it." (p. 24) This early uneasiness arose even though the majority of biblical Jews probably ate little meat if, in accordance with Mosaic law, they partook of meat mainly during the sacrifices held at the Temple during the pilgrimage festivals of Passover, Shevuot, and Sukkot. The laws in Leviticus 17:3-4 forbade killing an animal for food anywhere except upon the designated altar. As Schochet states, regulating the

7

consumption of meat by the necessity of sacrifice imposed "considerable restrictions." (p. 47)

The rabbis granted that meat had nutritional value, but the important issue was whether meat was necessary. Ice cream might be nutritional, but it is not a necessary nutritional food. Rashi's comment on the food riots in Exodus that "It was right for the Jews to cry for bread, but not for meat, for one can live without meat," reflects the distinction between necessary and unnecessary. As noted above, meat in the Bible is regarded as a food "of lust," not as necessary food. Discussions in the Talmud indicate that though the rabbis believed meat had nutritional value, they regarded it negatively, particularly after the Temple fell and the sacrificial system which, at least, restricted and lent dignity to the consumption of meat, came to an end.

"Man shall not eat meat unless he has a special craving for it, and shall eat it only occasionally and sparingly." (Chulin 84a)

A man should not teach his son to eat meat. (Chulin 84a)

Whether meat or any meat products (eggs and dairy) are necessary depends upon the total food environment. Under extreme situations of crop failures or vegetation deprivation, such as prevailed after Noah's flood and in times of famine, meat may be an expeditious way to stave off starvation, but the argument from necessity should apply only to dire circumstances.

Of course, the diet of rich biblical Jews was different from the diet of the poor. Oded Schwartz (*In Search of Plenty: A History of Jewish Food*) believes that the rich may have eaten meat two or three times a week in the biblical era, while the poor probably ate meat only several times a year. Diet is a barometer of wealth, like cars and jewelry. Meat has always been associated with wealth and for this reason attracted the bitter criticism of the prophets who understood its divisive nature. The meat of the sacrificed animals was eaten by the Temple priests, who apparently glutted themselves on it so that a special medical officer was needed to attend to the bowel sickness caused by their overindulgence. (John Cooper, *Eat and Be Satisfied*, p. 4) Isaiah's disgust with this meat gluttony goes hand in hand with his criticism of the sacrificial system and his concern for the poor.

Nevertheless, for rich or poor, there never has been a commandment in Judaism to eat meat. The diet of biblical Jews was enshrined as the "seven sacred foods of eretz Israel": wheat, barley, grapes, figs, pomegranates, olives, honey (from dates). Why then did the rabbis not advocate vegetarianism? Probably because they feared making a break with the long tradition of animal sacrifice, and because the vegetarianism of past cultures was often associated with alien concepts, such as celibacy and the condemnation of creation and matter, concepts which deny Judaism's basic impulses: choose life, be fruitful and multiply.

Another important decree in the laws of Moses, which had far-reaching effects, is the commandment, "thou shalt not seethe a kid in its mother's milk." This commandment, which is mentioned on three different occasions (Ex 23:19, 34:36, Deut. 14:21) has received endless commentary by both Jewish and non-Jewish scholars. Oded Schwartz calls it "...the most curious law of all." (It is interesting to note that in Genesis 18:8 Abraham and Sarah serve a meal of milk and meat to the visiting angels.) The commandment has echoes in other cultures, particularly African cultures, but similar statements also appear in the Pre-Socratic writings, where it is associated with deification of a mortal and with immortality:

"'Happy and blessed one, you shall be a god instead of a mortal.' I have fallen as a kid into milk." (Thuris, 4-3rd cent. BCE)

Speculations concerning this commandment are endless, but Philo of Alexandria gave the commandment its definitive Jewish interpretation when he declared that to seethe a kid in its mother's milk was morally repulsive because it is "improper that the matter which sustained the living animal should be used to flavour its meat after its death." Later rabbinic commentary declared that the prohibition was intended to refine our appetites with respect to meat. The prohibition underwent intensive expansion from 200-420 C.E., and the interpretations of this law, as of other laws concerning kashrut, became ethical and moral: concern for the animal and concern to refine human sensibility with respect to life.

In the modern world human consumption of meat has increased a thousandfold, and respect for animal life has almost vanished. Kashrut has not achieved what the rabbis declared was its purpose: to limit our consumption of meat and to encourage compassion for animal life. "...Reverence for Life...is the constant lesson of the laws of Kashrut." (Dresner, p. 27), but kashrut, as Dresner states, lacks "a satisfying modern formulation of its meaning and relevance" (p. 11). Jewish vegetarianism restores kashrut to its original intentions and its original simplicity, where purpose and practice have a relationship and harmony that can easily be grasped. Jewish vegetarianism stems from the positive, life-affirming Jewish values to guard one's health, protect the environment and revere life. The Union of American Hebrew Congregations' edition of The Torah, states the issue succinctly:

"In a larger sense we must rethink the whole question of eating, in view of our frequent statements that Judaism deals with every aspect of human life. Is it true that "a man is what he eats"? In what sense and in what degree?

Some Jews of widely varied religious backgrounds have become vegetarians on principle. Perhaps it is time to examine the question: Is it right to kill any living thing for food?" (1981 edition, p. 813)

Jewish vegetarianism contains a moral symmetry in its concern for human health, for animal life, for nature. It reaches down into the deepest level of moral insight that what is good for human health is good for the health of the planet and for other life on it. As Rabbi Arthur Green has stated it with moral urgency in his book, *Seek My Face, Speak My Name,*

"If Jews have to be associated with killing at all in our time, let it be only for the defense of human life. Life has become too precious in this era for us to be involved in the shedding of blood, even that of animals, when we can survive without it. This is not an ascetic choice, we should note, but rather a life-affirming one. A Jewish vegetarianism would be more whole in its ability to embrace the presence of God in all of Creation."

After The Fall of The Temple, and Onward

The dietary laws received their greatest expansion during Talmudic times. Louis Berman argues that after the fall of the Temple, "the dietary laws of the diaspora emerged as a replacement for the sacrificial system," and that "the Temple priest was replaced by the diaspora shochet."
(Vegetarianism and The Jewish Tradition, p. 27)

Since eating meat was historically embedded in the sacrificial system after the Temple fell there was much discussion in the Talmud about what the status of meat should now be. The association of eating meat with the festivals bequeathed to the Jews the tradition that joyous occasions (*simchat yom tov*) should be celebrated with meat and wine. However, this association with meat was declared no longer to be in effect after the sacrifices ended. A Talmudic text states: "In the days when the Temple was in existence, there was no rejoicing without meat...but now that there is no longer the Temple, there is no rejoicing without wine...." (Rabbi Judah ben Betairah in *Beit Yoseph*). Jews are commanded to celebrate the holidays with wine and with joy, but there is no halachic requirement to celebrate it with meat.

After the fall of the Temple the focus of Jewish celebration shifted from the Temple to the synagogue and the home. The table in one's home, prepared properly for Shabbat, the holidays, was considered to be an altar. Rabbi Moshe Iserlis declared, "The table is like an altar and the meal is an offering." (Hilcot B'tziyat Hapat, 167:5) It was a brilliant shift, testifying to the flexibility of the rabbis who were able to take command of the historic necessities of the hour and recast the locus of the Jewish religion from the Temple to the home, where every Jew could officiate over the commandments for holiness.

"Today we have no Temple in Jerusalem, no altar there, no sacrifices, no priests to minister. But in their stead we have something even greater. For every home can be a Temple, every table an altar, every meal a sacrifice and every Jew a priest." (Dresner, p. 40)

Since the blessings over food are required for the sanctification of eating, there is much discussion in *Talmud Berakhot* about foods and their values. All things which are enjoyed require a blessing; to enjoy without blessing the Creator is likened to theft. "Rab Judah said in the name of Samuel: To enjoy anything of this world without a benediction is like making personal use of things consecrated to heaven, since it says, The earth is the Lord's and the fullness thereof." (35d) The model for the blessings is produce from the earth, and of these the perfect model are the seven foods of the land (35a ff.): wheat, barley, vines, pomegranates, figs, olives, and honey.

"For the Lord Thy God brings thee into a good land, a land of water courses, of fountains and depths that spring out of valleys and hills; a land of wheat and barley and vines and fig trees and pomegranates; a land of olive oil and honey; a land in which thou shalt eat bread without scarceness, thou shalt not lack any thing in it." (Deut. 8: 8-9)

Modern Realities: Some Unpalatable Facts

One does not have to go as far back as the biblical diet to discover the simplicity of kashrut in some of its original format. A hundred years ago before chemically transformed foods became common, except for the few laws concerning meat and meat products (eggs and dairy), and the mixing of meat and milk, fruits and vegetables naturally grown were naturally kosher. A kosher diet was a natural diet--that was when we knew what "natural" meant, before industrialization overtook our food, and before animals were fed antibiotics, pesticides and hormones; before "shelf life" in the supermarket became the necessary goal of breeders, which requires that problems of packaging, transporting, refrigerating and preserving become food issues. A shtetl housewife did not need to know how to read to know what was kosher. She did not need a label to guide her with respect to produce. Nature guided her. If she was in doubt she asked her rabbi.

Today many of us feel that we need an advanced degree in chemistry to go shopping. Moreover, trust in the labels--when you can decipher them--

11

has broken down because the rules change constantly as the processing systems change, and as food becomes more technologically engineered. Trust in the foods we eat has all but evaporated. We do not know what is "safe" and "not safe;" much less "clean" and "not clean." There are over a hundred different kosher labels listed by *Kashrus Magazine* (November, 1994). Rabbi Lipschutz' compilation and designation of food additives is forty pages long. (*Kashrut: A Comprehensive Background and Reference Guide to the Principles of Kashrut*)

For Jews, living in urban centers as most people in industrialized societies do, a label of "kosher" no longer simplifies, but adds to the complexity, for the label, particularly when it comes to meat, does not necessarily reflect any more health, safety or mercy than other labels. "Kosher" meat reflects a technical ritual determination of how the animal was killed and whether there were certain proscribed blemishes on its lungs. A "blemish" defined halachically, does not convey information about the hormones and pesticides that were fed to the animal, and whether or not the animal was irradiated or genetically altered. Kosher food animals, except for a few Jewish farming communities who raise their own animals, are raised the same way that all commercially raised food animals are.

The problem of meat and meat products in the modern world is unprecedented, kosher or not. Past civilizations, whether hunting, pastoral or agricultural, ate meat rarely and almost never all year around, for meat could not be kept in warm weather. The rise in consumption of meat as a daily habit began in the West in the later Middle Ages and reached its critical peak in this century, when we have possibly consumed more meat than was consumed in all past centuries put together. This rise in meat consumption has been accompanied by a steady decrease in the consumption of essential foods such as vegetables and grains, so that our diet has undergone the most revolutionary change since human beings appeared on the earth. For the past 10,000 years or so, the human race in its upright posture lived on a carbohydrate-plant-based diet. Modern Western people are the first people in history to have a meat-protein based diet. Eating meat on a daily basis is a modern phenomenon, brought about by technological improvements in transportation (trains, ships, trucks), refrigeration and freezing. The historic problem with meat (as with fish) has always been that it deteriorates quickly and its rapid deterioration can be dangerous. Its shelf life is practically nil, and adulteration is easily camouflaged.

The enormous increase in meat consumption occurred simultaneously with the development of a sedentary way of life in climate-controlled environments which has probably slowed our metabolic rates. During this same century which saw the unprecedented change in diet, U.S. rates of chronic diseases increased dramatically. Death rates from cancer tripled and death rates from heart disease doubled. The leading causes of death in the U.S. related to diet are heart disease, cancer, stroke and diabetes.

The diseases associated with over-consumption of meat are the diseases of affluent nations. Throughout history, status rather than necessity, has influenced what and how much food is eaten. Often when a food loses status it is fed to animals, as soybeans are in this country, and it is then considered degrading for human consumption. Sometimes the diet of the poor is sounder than the diet of the rich, as in the use of black bread and brown rice by the poor, in contrast to the consumption of white bread and polished white rice by the rich. (Ironically, it is now the affluent and knowledgeable who eat whole grain breads and brown rice, and the poor and uneducated who eat white bread and white rice.) Nutritional value and rational choices have little to do with diet. Status and habit are the great determinants, not health or even pleasure, for people often work hard at acquiring a taste for something they prefer not to eat. Many children have a natural aversion to meat. They have to be socialized into eating it and can only swallow it if it is cooked to shoe leather consistency and smothered with ketchup.

In the United States, the impact of a high meat diet upon our health care costs has been so corrosive that medical expenses related to meat eating threaten millions of people. A study by The Physician's Committee for Responsible Medicine in *The New York Times,* reported by Jane Brody (November 21, 1995), estimated that "the yearly national health care costs of eating meat are comparable to the estimated $50 billion spent each year to treat illnesses related to smoking." It is immoral for a rich nation to contemplate health care rationing; it is immoral for young people who lack the discipline to curb their appetites, to calculate the medical costs of keeping their elderly parents alive.

Nothing is so wasteful in nature as our present diet. It is a chief cause of environmental pollution. In countries where animals are "factory farmed," or raised with intensive rearing methods in feedlots, the antibiotics and chemicals used in the production of meat runs off into rivers and streams and pollutes them with dangerous chemicals. Excrement from livestock in general is 250,000 pounds per second, compared with 12,000 pounds per second for the human population. In the United States, where meat consumption is high, this animal excrement is a moving storehouse of toxic waste, pesticides, hormones and antibiotics. Antibiotics fed to the animals do not go away. They are flushed into the ground, into our waters, and on to our vegetables and fruit. In 1988, the Environmental Protection Agency blamed agricultural runoff for the most extensive source of pollution. Additionally, the methane gases produced by cows contribute to about 15% of the greenhouse effect.

These problems have been developing since after the second World War, when a system of husbandry evolved which is called "factory farming." This term is used because the presumptions of efficiency and marketing are those of the factory assembly belt, except that in this case the "end product" is a living animal, not a machine, not a tool, not a car, not a razor blade, not a *thing,* but an originally born creature born of a born creature. But this creature is called an "animal *machine.*" What becomes of a civilization that cannot distinguish between "thing" or "machine" and "born creature"? How far does a creature have to be transformed before it is a thing, and how shall we designate its proper blessing: for creature or thing?

Jeremy Rifkin in his book, *Beyond Beef,* points out that our traditional morality framed by the Ten Commandments, cannot address the institutionalized evil of factory farming. "What of evil born of rationalized methods of discourse, scientific objectivity, mechanistic reductionism, utilitarianism, and market efficiency?....A new dimension of evil...has been incorporated into the modern cattle complex--a cold evil that flows from the very Enlightenment principles that animate much of the modern world view." (p. 283-284) Neither can traditional Jewish blessings or concepts of kashrut, as formulated up to now, address the animal machine. Rabbi David Rosen has declared, "...meat consumption has become halachically unjustifiable." (*Rabbis and Vegetarianism,* p.54) The farm animal is the first victim in the blurring line between human being and machine that has accompanied progress since the Enlightenment, and it mocks Genesis.

Since the Second World War, there has also been a parade of books and studies warning us against the moral and health hazards of today's meat. *Animal Machines* by Ruth Harrison in 1964 carried a Foreword by Rachel Carson, with a warning:

"As a biologist whose special interests lie in the field of ecology, or the relation between living things and their environment, I find it inconceivable that healthy animals can be produced under the artificial and damaging conditions that prevail in these modern factory-like installations, where animals are grown and turned out like so many inanimate objects....Diseases sweep through these establishments, which indeed are kept going only by the continuous administration of antibiotics. Disease organisms then become resistant to the antibiotics. Veal calves purposely kept in a state of induced anaemia so their white flesh will satisfy the supposed desires of the gourmet, sometimes drop dead when taken out of their imprisoning crates."

Exploitation of animals for food is not new, but the exploitation has become relentless, without surcease in the animal's life. As Ruth Harrison wrote, "It has been taken to a degree where the animal is not allowed to live before it dies." Or as one protest poster declaimed: "Before this animal is slaughtered, it will wish it had never been born." Rabbi Rosen declares, as have the Jewish sages throughout the centuries: "The explicit purpose of the biblical dietary laws is holiness...." (*Rabbis and Vegetarianism*, p. 54) Where is holiness in this meat? Where is respect for creation? Where is plain compassion? From the point of view of the veal calf lying in its own manure in a dark crate for weeks on end, without sunshine or wind or rain or grass or smell or warmth or sound, there never was a creation.

Social justice depends on sound ecological principles which use the land in the most productive and equitable manner possible. Meat wastes the land and violates the Jewish value of *bal tashchit* , which commands us not to be wasteful and to use everything in nature with loving prudence. Torah and Talmud are filled with ecological concerns. The frequent metaphor in prophetic writing, "the seed of peace" was the prophets' proverbial term for these agricultural values.

Samuel Dresner has observed that "Philosophy and diet go hand in hand." For the Jew, philosophy and diet, religion and history go hand in hand. We see, now, after we peel away the layers of incremental habits and laws that have accumulated to protect the original instinct of kashrut that there is no surer and better way to follow it than by becoming a vegetarian. It is the historical fulfillment of our dietary commandments, a new dietary ethic which resolves the conflict between modernity and traditional kashrut. Vegetarianism can restore respect for the lives of non-human creatures and the sense of the holiness of creation. The Jewish arguments for vegetarianism today are manifold: for human health, for environmental health, for moral health. It is a cry for life. Jewish vegetarianism asks: is this food hazardous to human health? Is this food the product of cruelty? Does eating this food destroy the Jewish concept of nature and of a merciful Creator?

Modern Realities: Some Palatable Facts

The time has never been more propitious for a diet that is enticing, healthy and plausible. Due to modern communication, culinary offerings today draw upon every culture. Vegetarian cookbooks matured with the use of fascinating recipes and ingredients from around the world. The Jewish diet likewise has been enriched by the diaspora, by cooking habits and recipes that Jews have taken with them around the world. But what we consider to be a "traditional" Jewish dish is often not older than a century or a century and a half, and reflects other currents in Jewish life. A Jewish cookbook published in England in 1846 has no references to bagels, lox, gefilte fish, borscht or mentions "cholent" (foods of Eastern European Jews), but contains Sephardic and Dutch dishes, since many Jews living in England at that time were Sephardic Jews who had come from Holland. For most Eastern European Jews during the 17th, 18th and 19th centuries, famine, the fear of famine influenced their diet and their attitude towards food. In the nineteenth century, the potato, with its high nutritive value, became as important to Ashkenazi Jews as it was to the Irish, and the East European diet added many potato recipes. Jews, like other people, often found interesting ways to vary a modest diet or a diet defined by religious restrictions. The invention of the cholent and tzimmis, which can simmer throughout the Shabbat, are examples of this. The most consistent tradition in Jewish cooking is the idea of holiday food as festive and special. This is what we hope our recipes express: the traditional Jewish holiday spirit of simchat yom tov, with dishes that evoke the symbolism and seasons of the holidays.

For this we have drawn on the Ashkenazic and Sephardic traditions, and on recipes that generations of Jewish families have enjoyed in the New World. Wherever Jews lived, they adapted native dishes to their needs, and when they moved they took with them the foods they had learned to love.

These menus are designed for holiday feasting. Even though they are vegan some are richer than your everyday fare. For those concerned about weight, there are ways to reduce fat in these recipes with substitutes. Except in baking, you can reduce the amount of oil by using non-stick cookware, a vegetarian spray and/or by "sweating" the onions and other chopped vegetables. (See Appendix article on Oil.) In general, it is advisable to follow a low-fat diet, but holiday food, like holiday clothes, should be special.

We have chosen recipes that are delicious, varied, but generally not labor intensive. All are vegan and can be integrated into any meal. Our aim in this cookbook is to make it easier to maintain kashrut, but if processed foods are substituted for fresh foods they may or may not be pareve, depending upon the degree of transformation which has taken place in the food. (See Appendix article, "Vegetarian, Vegan, Pareve") A guide to this problem can be found in Dresner's book, *The Jewish Dietary Laws* [p. 96-99], or a rabbinic authority should be consulted. To make holiday preparations easier, many dishes can be made in advance. Most ingredients should be available in local supermarkets. Some ingredients may require a trip to a health food store or to an ethnic market, which can be a culinary treasure hunt. Becoming a vegetarian is an adventure in food, spices, herbs and culinary history. Discovering new ingredients makes cooking and eating fascinating. Go boldly forth and experiment. It's almost impossible to ruin a vegetarian dish, unless you overcook it or smother it in oil.

These recipes are flexible, and can be changed and worked into a family's needs. They are flavorful, but not highly spiced by today's standards. Feel free to increase or reduce the spices by adjusting the amounts of pepper, vinegar, curry, cumin, etc., or to use other spices than the ones suggested here. The recipes in this cookbook are not engraved in stone. Adjust them to your tastes and needs. You can chop vegetables, grill them, sauté them, steam them, boil them, mash them, bake them, cook them in a skillet, in a wok, in a double-boiler, a pressure cooker, a micro-wave oven, or a traditional oven. You can cook fruits and vegetables together, such as green peppers and apples, grated beets and grated apples, or grated carrots with raisins. The possibilities are practically endless and up to you, your taste, your passion, and your pocketbook. If cinnamon offends your family, leave it out. If cumin or curry are your favorite spices, try them on anything. Reach out for the vegetable, fruit, grain, herb and spice world around you.

Where the dishes are rich, we recommend a plain bread, but if you are ambitious, place one rich bread and one simple bread on the table. In general, a green salad with an oil and vinegar dressing goes with any meal. Fresh herbs like basil or dill will bring more magic to your salad than commercial dressings.

Before using this cookbook, read the information in the appendices for terms, hints, and suggestions which might make your work easier. You are the cook and this is your cookbook, a vegetarian cookbook for festivals and holidays, for *simchat yom tov,* so that you can experience how deeply related the Jewish calendar is to the seasons and to the biblical agricultural cycles. The holidays often seem to appear unexpectedly. That's because we compute them in relation to the Roman calendar used in the Western world. In the Jewish calendar they always fall in the same month, in relation to a specific season or an agricultural activity. We are reminded everyday in the Sh'ma of the closeness of our trust in God to agricultural blessing:

> *If you will earnestly heed the mitzvot that I give you this day, to love the Lord your God and to serve God with all your heart and all your soul, then I will favor your land with rain at the proper season--rain in the autumn and rain in spring--and you will have an ample harvest of grain, wine and oil.* (Deut. 11:13-15)

The Table As Altar

For the Jew there are five good reasons not to eat meat: tsa'ar ba'alei chayim (remember the pain of living creatures), pikuach nefesh (human health), bal tashchit (do not waste the world), tzeddakah (meat robs the poor), and klal Israel (the community of Jews): vegetarianism allows all Jews to sit down at the same table. Food is still the best social cement there is. Where the table and household are vegetarian, where the cooking pots, dishes, and utensils have never known meat or meat products, Jews of every kind can eat together in the spirit of klal Israel.

The Jewish holidays chronicle the seasons. So should the Jewish table, if we eat in relation to the Jewish calendar. The holidays are a garland that weave nature, Jewish history, and ritual together.

It is traditional to wash one's hands before eating and to remain silent until the b'racha is said. It is a good time to meditate on the words from our Sages: "All your deeds should be for the sake of heaven, even things of choice, such as eating and drinking." Bread and wine are regarded as sacred and we say blessings over them. It is rare for knives to be on a table where vegetarian food is served but if they are, they are removed after the meal and before grace is said, so that there are no implements of violence at this time. On Shabbat the candles grace the table, which bring a mellow light to the room. They soften voices and the spirit, which modernity often makes strident.

Isaiah believed that the significant blessing of our gracious God Who has given us abundance from the earth was, "May you eat the good things of the earth." And so we bless the food that grows from the earth:

For vegetables that grow from the ground:

We bless You , Eternal Source of Creation,
Who creates the vegetables of the ground

For fruit or vegetables that are chopped or mashed:

We bless You , Eternal Source of Creation,
through Whose Word everything happens

For the fruit from a new crop:

We bless you , Eternal source of Creation, for keeping us alive,
taking care of us and bringing us to this season.

B'tay-avon--- and may you eat the good things of the earth.

Helpful Hints Before You Cook

1. Before starting to cook, read recipe through, noting ingredients, equipment, time and procedures involved.

2. Assemble and measure ingredients before starting to combine them, especially when baking.

3. Note that the number of servings and size of portions depend on the number of dishes on a menu. An entrée enough for 10-12 for a gala buffet may feed 8 as part of a less lavish menu.

4. Vegetable oil means any bland oil of your choice: canola, safflower, peanut, corn, but not olive. Margarine means any vegan/pareve margarine.

5. Raw chopped onions can be frozen. You can prepare quantities ahead of time and save time later. Frozen onions should be used only in cooked dishes.

6. When cooking garlic, do not let it brown. Browned garlic has an unpleasant taste. Our recipes include a separate step of cooking the garlic for a minute after onions and peppers are tender.

7. Use fresh produce and herbs. If the available herbs you need look tired, choose another herb or, where possible, use dried herbs if fresh herbs cannot be had: 1 teaspoon dried for 1 tablespoon fresh. Do not use dried mint.

8. Wash all vegetables before cutting them, even if they are organic. Organic produce can have dust and other particles on them.

9. Good slicing and chopping technique--"knife skills"--are essential. They make your work faster and easier. If necessary, have a skilled friend demonstrate them for you, or take a cooking class that teaches them.

10. Our menus are meant to be helpful and appropriate to the holidays and their seasons, but feel free to rearrange them to suit your preferences and needs.

11. It is both economical and healthier to eat foods in season. Though it is not always possible to do this, try your best.

12. Less than perfect fruits and vegetables are not only economical, but often taste good, and can be used quite wonderfully in compotes and stews.

SHABBAT

A Winter Shabbat Menu

Golden Glow Shabbat Soup
or Velvety Green Pea Soup
Stuffed Cabbage in Sweet and Sour Sauce
or Hot Meatless Loaf
Mixed Green Salad
Israeli Winter Fruit Cup

A Spring Shabbat Menu

Leek and Potato Soup
Bean and Barley Cholent
Broccoli Vinaigrette
Mediterranean Tomato Salad
Applesauce Cake

A Summer Shabbat Menu

Cold Curried Split Pea Soup
Asparagus With Sweet Red Peppers
Meatless Loaf, Cold
Dill and Green Olive Potato Salad
Peach Tart

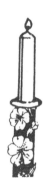

Recipes for Shabbat At A Glance:
Challah
Appetizer: Spinach Dip
Soup: Vegetable Stock, Golden Glow Shabbat Soup, Leek and Potato Soup, Cold Curried Green Pea Soup, Velvety Green Pea Soup
Entrées: Bean and Barley Cholent, Meatless Loaf, Stuffed Cabbage With Kasha, Kasha With Bow Ties
Side Dish: Irish Colcannon
Salads: Mediterranean Tomato Salad, Dill and Green Olive Potato Salad
Vegetables Asparagus With Red Peppers, Broccoli Vinaigrette,
Desserts: Peach Tart, Applesauce Cake, Chocolate Cake, Israeli Winter Fruit Cup

"He received the Sabbath with sweet song and chanted the hallowing tunefully over raisin wine; while it was still day and the sun came to gaze at his glass ....The table was well spread with all manner of fruit, beans, green stuffs and good pies, plum water tasting like wine, but of flesh and fish there was never a sign....In truth it is in no way obligatory to eat flesh and fish. The old man and his wife had never tasted flesh since growing to maturity....That old man was one of the Thirty-six Hidden Saints upon whom the whole world rests, and can therefore be presumed to have known what is acceptable to Him, may He be blessed."   S.Y. Agnon, *The Bridal Canopy*

"On the Sabbath it is given us to share in the holiness that is in the heart of time. Even when the soul is seared, even when no prayer can come out of our tightened throats, the clean, silent rest of the Sabbath leads us to a realm of endless peace, or to the beginning of an awareness of what eternity means. There are few ideas in the world of thought which contain so much spiritual power as the idea of the Sabbath. Aeons hence, when of many of our cherished theories only shreds will remain, that cosmic tapestry will continue to shine."
          Abraham Joshua Heschel, *The Sabbath: Its Meaning for Modern Man*

Challah

Everyone knows that challah is the indispensable bread for Shabbat in the majority of Ashkenazic homes. Other communities have their own special Shabbat loaves. All trace their origins to the shewbread that God commanded the priests to place on the shewtable in the Temple.(Num. 15:19-20; Ex. 25:30). While we do not know that recipe for the shewbread, it is unlikely that it contained eggs as do many modern versions. In honor of the double portion of manna which God provided for the wandering Israelites, every Shabbat we place two loaves of challah on our table.

When baking challah, it is obligatory to remove a small amount of dough--a piece about the size of an olive--before shaping the loaves. Just before baking the challahs, this little piece is tossed into the hot oven and the baker says the following blessing in memory of the offerings in Temple days:

Blessed are You, Lord our God, Ruler of the universe, Who has sanctified us with your commandments, and has commanded us to separate the challah.

This ceremony is called "taking challah." While both men and women perform it, it is one of the three mitzvot, along with lighting the Sabbath candles and ritual immersion in the mikveh, that are special for women.

The following challah recipe was prepared for a demonstration in the kitchen of Temple Sinai in Marblehead, Massachusetts by Chelly Goldberg, whose husband Jonas Goldberg is the rabbi of Temple Sinai. Chelly prepared a huge batch earlier in the day to use for a hands-on demonstration of braiding the dough. Sixteen women each braided a small challah, and while the bread baked Chelly made another batch of dough so that we could see how easily it was done. Meanwhile, the kitchen smelled like heaven. We could hardly wait until the loaves came out of the oven. And what a memorable sight they were! Sixteen golden, tender, fragrant, slightly lopsided, absolutely delicious challahs.

We adapted Chelly's recipe to the vegan kitchen, successfully using flaxseed and water to replace the eggs. If you have a favorite family recipe for challah, try it this way:

Challah

2 packages dry yeast
2 cups warm water (105-115 ^{0} F)
1/2 cup sugar, divided
3 tablespoons flaxseeds
3/4 cup water
6-9 cups unbleached white flour
2 tablespoons honey
2 teaspoons salt
3 ounces vegetable oil
1/2 teaspoon turmeric
Raisins (optional,
    but include for Rosh Hashanah challah)

In a small bowl, dissolve yeast in 2 cups warm water. (Use a thermometer, if possible. Otherwise, add 1 cup boiling water to 1 cup cold water.) Add 1/4 cup sugar, and allow the yeast to work for about 10 minutes while you prepare the dry ingredients.

Place flaxseeds and water in a blender and blend for about 2 minutes or until the mixture is the consistency of unbeaten egg white. Or grind the seeds in a spice mill or coffee grinder; place ground seeds and water in bowl of food processor and beat to desired consistency.

Place 6 cups flour, salt, remaining sugar and raisins (if using) in a large bowl. Add flaxseed mixture, oil, honey and yeast. Mix until dough forms, adding more flour if needed. Turn the dough out onto a floured surface, flour your hands and knead the dough for about 10 minutes. Add flour as necessary until the dough no longer sticks to the board or your hands.

Oil a deep bowl. Put the dough in it, turning to grease it on all sides. Cover the bowl with a damp cloth or with plastic wrap, and allow to rise for about 1-1/2 hours, or until doubled in bulk.

Punch down and allow to rise a second time. Punch down again and knead briefly. Use a heavy, sharp knife to cut the dough in half. Cover one half while you shape the first loaf.

Oil a baking sheet. Divide one dough ball into three equal parts. Roll each one into a "snake," using a back and forth motion and keeping the dough under the palms of your hands. Each "snake" should be about 16" long. Allow them to rest a few minutes, then pinch the three strands together at one end, braid them, and pinch them together at the other end. (Continued)

Remove the first loaf to an oiled baking sheet. Shape the second loaf, place it on the baking sheet, and allow the loaves to rise again.

Preheat oven to 350^0 F.

For a crisp crust, brush loaves with cold water before placing in oven. Bake 25-35 minutes. The usual criterion for doneness is that the loaf sounds hollow when rapped on the bottom with your knuckles, or you may insert a thermometer in a crease on the bottom of the bread. It should register 200^0 F.

Cool loaves on a cooling rack. Makes 2 large loaves. Freezes well.

Preparation tip: You can make the dough the evening before and refrigerate it after the first or second rising. Extra dough can also be used for dinner rolls.

To form round challahs for Rosh Hashanah, and the first Shabbat of each month: Divide the dough in two balls. Roll each one into a thick rope and coil the rope upon itself. If you prefer, divide the dough in thirds and make 3 loaves.

Spinach Dip

Don't like spinach? Don't like tofu? Our data show that everyone loves this dip. Should be made several hours ahead for flavors to blend.

> 1 10 ounce package frozen chopped spinach,
>   thawed and drained
> 1 cup soy mayonnaise
> 1/2 pound soft tofu, cut in chunks
> 1/2 cup minced green onion
> 1/2 cup minced parsley
> 1 teaspoon fresh dill
> 1/2 teaspoon salt
> Lemon juice to taste

Serve with cut-up fresh vegetables and/or toasted pita triangles for dipping, or spread on your challah.

Squeeze spinach to remove moisture. In food processor, combine tofu and mayonnaise and process until blended. Add remaining ingredients, and process until smooth. Chill well.

Note: If made the day before serving, use more dill or add more dill just before serving, as this flavor fades.

Some good vegetables for dipping are peppers of all colors, carrots, cucumbers, cauliflower and broccoli. Cut peppers and carrots into sticks, cut cauliflower and broccoli into florets. Slice cucumbers.

To make toasted pita triangles: cut a pita into 2 rounds, stack them, and cut into triangles. Heat in 350^0 F. oven 5-10 minutes, until golden brown.

Vegetable Stock

An invaluable asset to have on hand.

2 Spanish onions, chopped
2 leeks, white and light green parts, chopped
2 large carrots, in chunks
2 celery ribs, in chunks
28 ounce can crushed Italian tomatoes
4 bay leaves
10 large parsley sprigs
10 thyme springs
2 teaspoons whole black peppercorns
4 quarts water

Combine all ingredients in large stock pot. Bring to a boil; adjust heat and simmer, uncovered, about 1 1/2 hours. Skim the foam from the stock as necessary.

Strain through a fine sieve, pressing down firmly on vegetables with the back of a spoon to extract all the juices and flavors. Discard solids. Makes about 3 quarts.

If not using stock immediately, freeze in containers of various sizes--1 cup, 1 pint, 1 quart-- for your future convenience.

Golden Glow Shabbat Soup

1 pound package (2 cups dry) yellow split peas
1 cup grated parsnips
1 cup grated carrots
Salt to taste
3 bay leaves

Cook yellow split peas according to directions on package.
Halfway through cooking time, add parsnips, carrots, salt and bay leaves.
Simmer with partially covered lid. Remove bay leaves before serving.
For a golden color and smoother taste, purée. Serves 8.

Leek and Potato Soup

2 large leeks, trimmed and cleaned, white parts only
1 pound Yukon gold potatoes, peeled, cut in 1/4" dice
2 tablespoons margarine
1 cup finely chopped onions
3 cups vegetable stock
2 cups water
1 bay leaf
Salt and freshly ground pepper to taste
Minced fresh chives

Chop leeks in 1/4" lengths. Melt margarine in 3 quart or larger saucepan. Add onions and leeks. Cook over medium heat until golden and limp. Add potatoes, stock, water, bay leaf, salt and pepper. Bring to simmer and cook for 30 minutes, or until potatoes are tender.

Discard bay leaf. Use a potato masher to partly mash potatoes; if you prefer a thicker, smoother soup, put soup in processor fitted with steel blade and pulse until desired thickness. Correct seasonings. Garnish with chives. Serves 4-6.

Preparation Tip: You can use other varieties of potato, but the Yukon Gold gives the soup a rich golden color appropriate for Shabbat and holidays. If you want the soup to keep its golden color, serve the same day.

Cold Curried Green Pea Soup

Chilled soups are lovely to serve for a summer Shabbat evening.

1 pound package (2 cups dry) split green peas
1 medium onion, chopped
1/2 cup chopped celery
1 teaspoon salt, or to taste
2 teaspoons curry powder, or to taste

Cook according to directions on green pea package. When soup is done, add curry. Cool, then purée in blender. Chill about 2 hours. Serves 6-8.

Velvety Green Pea Soup

A green pea soup for chillier nights.
This soup is as smooth, subtle and elegant as its name implies.

1 tablespoon vegetable oil
1 1/2 cups chopped onions
2 teaspoons crushed garlic
2 carrots, peeled and chopped
1/2 pound mushrooms, sliced
6 cups vegetable stock
2 medium potatoes, peeled and diced
2 (20 ounce) bags frozen sweet peas
        (about 6 cups) divided
1 cup corn kernels, fresh or frozen
1 1/2 teaspoons dried rosemary
1 1/2 teaspoons dried thyme
Salt to taste

In a 4 quart non stick saucepan, heat oil. Sauté onions, mushrooms and carrots until just tender, about 5 minutes. Add garlic and sauté one minute more. add stock, potatoes, and all but 1/2 cup of the peas. Simmer, covered, for 20-25 minutes, or until potatoes are tender, adjusting heat as necessary.

In food processor, purée soup until perfectly smooth. Reheat, adding herbs, corn, and remaining peas. Serves 8.

Note: Can be made early in the day and refrigerated until ready to serve. Reheat gently.

Irish Colcannon

Chances are that Robert Briscoe (1894-1969), Dublin's Jewish Lord Mayor, ate his fair share of this hearty, warming dish during a lifetime as an Irish patriot and politician. It reminds us that potatoes and cabbage were essential staples for Eastern European Jews as they were for the Irish.

3 Idaho potatoes, peeled and diced
1/2 small green cabbage, shredded
1/2 cup soy milk
1 teaspoon kosher salt
Freshly ground pepper
1 tablespoon margarine

Boil or steam potatoes and cabbage separately until tender.
In a large bowl, mash the potatoes with a potato masher, adding soy milk a little at a time until the potatoes are creamy.

Add remaining ingredients and combine.
Taste for salt and pepper and correct seasonings if necessary.
Serve hot. Serves 6-8.

Bean and Barley Cholent

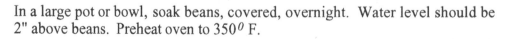

1/2 pound Great Northern beans
1/4 cup vegetable oil
2 large onions, chopped
1 large carrot, sliced thin
3 cloves garlic, chopped
1 tablespoon sweet paprika
1 tablespoon honey
1/2 cup pearl barley
5 cups boiling water
Salt and freshly ground pepper to taste

In a large pot or bowl, soak beans, covered, overnight. Water level should be 2" above beans. Preheat oven to 350^0 F.

Heat oil in a large, heavy oven casserole. Add onions, sauté until golden.
Stir in sliced carrot, cook 5 more minutes.
Stir in garlic and cook 1 more minute.
Remove vegetables with a slotted spoon, drain well and set aside.

Stir in paprika and honey. Return vegetables to pot. Stir in barley.
Drain beans and add them to pot.

Add boiling water, cover and bake for 30 minutes. Reduce heat to 250^0, and bake 30 minutes longer. Remove cover and season with salt and pepper. Serves 4-6.

Meatless Loaf

Excellent choice for a Shabbat dinner. Can feed many, keeps well and can be served chilled the next day.

> 2 tablespoons vegetable oil
> 1 large onion, diced
> 1 cup chopped walnuts
> 1 cup rolled oats (not instant variety)
> 1/2 pound mushrooms, sliced
> 2 cups vegetable broth
>   (vegetable cubes can be used to make broth)
> 2 cloves garlic, minced
> 1 cup grated carrot
> 3 tablespoons Dijon, or other hearty mustard
> 4 tablespoons tomato sauce
> 2 tablespoons soy or tamari sauce
> 1 pound firm tofu, drained
> 2 tablespoons arrowroot powder
> 2 cups whole wheat bread crumbs,
>   or other preferred bread crumbs

Preheat oven to 375^0 F.
In a large skillet, heat 1 tablespoon oil. Sauté onion slowly until a rich brown, about 15 minutes. Stir occasionally. Transfer onions to a large mixing bowl.

In the same skillet, heat remaining oil, add walnuts, and sauté over medium heat 3 minutes. Add oats, sauté another 3 minutes, stirring. Add mushrooms, broth, and garlic. Reduce heat to low. Cook until mushrooms soften and stock is absorbed, about 8 minutes.

While oat mixture cooks, add carrot, mustard, tomato sauce, soy sauce or tamari. Add oat mixture to bowl with onions, and set aside. (Continued)

Purée tofu and arrowroot powder in blender or food processor until smooth. Add to oat-carrot mixture, and mix well. Add bread crumbs and mix again. Pour into oiled 5" x 2 3/4" loaf pan. Bake 40 minutes. Cool 30 minutes before slicing. Serves 8.

Stuffed Cabbage With Kasha

> 1 large head cabbage, about 3 pounds
> 1/4 cup oil
> 1 medium onion, finely chopped
> 2 cups kasha
> Salt and freshly ground pepper to taste
> 4 cups water
> 1 recipe tomato sauce

If you have time, freeze the cabbage head for two days. Thaw it overnight in a colander in the sink; the leaves will come apart easily and be pliable. Otherwise, bring a large pot of water to boil and cook the cabbage for about 5 minutes to soften the leaves. Drain and set aside in the colander.

Sauté the onion in the oil in a heavy 2 or 3 quart pot. Add the kasha, and turn it in the oil to coat all grains. Add salt, pepper and water. Bring to a boil, reduce heat, and simmer, covered, about 15 or 20 minutes. Check at 15 minutes. Remove from heat when just a small amount of water remains in the bottom of the pot. Let sit a few minutes until the kasha absorbs the water. Stir to fluff and separate the grains.

Preheat oven to 350⁰ F.
Separate the cabbage leaves. On each leaf, place 2 or 3 heaping tablespoons of kasha. Fold one edge of the leaf over the filling, tuck in the sides, and roll. Cut up any leftover cabbage, and place in an oiled baking dish or casserole. Place rolls seam side down on top. Pour in tomato sauce almost to cover. Cover with foil or lid and bake about 2 hours or until cabbage is tender. Uncover for the last 45 minutes to allow the sauce to thicken. Baste occasionally. Taste, and add more sugar or vinegar if necessary. Serves 8-10. *(Continued for Sauce)*

Sauce:

1 28 ounce can + 1 16 ounce can tomatoes
9 ounces tomato paste (1 1/2 6 ounce cans)
6 tablespoons brown sugar
6 tablespoons vinegar
rind of 1 1/2 oranges, grated (orange part only)
1 teaspoon salt, or to taste
1 1/2 teaspoons basil
Freshly ground black pepper to taste

Drain some liquid from the tomatoes into a heavy 3 quart pot. Stir in the tomato paste until smooth. Add remaining contents of tomato cans. Mash the tomatoes with a potato masher to break them up. Stir in the rest of the ingredients. Simmer about 10 minutes. Stir and add to baking pan. Proceed as above.

Kasha With Bow Ties

1-2 tablespoons oil
1 large or 2 small onions, chopped
1 1/2 cups kasha (buckwheat groats)
3 cups water
1 teaspoon salt
1/8 teaspoon freshly ground pepper
2 cups Italian bow tie noodles (farfalle)

In a large pot of boiling water, cook the bow ties according to package directions. Drain the pasta.

In a 3 quart saucepan, heat the oil over medium heat. Add the onion and sauté until tender and translucent. Remove onions from pot with a slotted spoon and reserve. Add kasha and stir a few minutes until grains become a little darker. Add water and salt and bring to a boil. Reduce heat and simmer covered, until most of the water is absorbed, about 12 minutes. Remove from heat and let stand, covered, about 5 minutes more. The kasha will absorb remaining water.

Stir in onions and pepper. Add pasta and mix gently. Correct seasonings. Serves 8-10.

Asparagus With Red Peppers

The seasonings here enhance the flavor of the asparagus without overwhelming it. Perfect for those who love asparagus and those who will after they taste this dish.

> 2 pounds asparagus
> 4 tablespoons vegetable oil
> 1 teaspoon salt, or to taste
> 4 garlic cloves, thinly sliced
> 1 cup water
> 2 red bell peppers, seeded, deribbed,
>   and cut into 2" long julienne
> 2 1/2 teaspoons cornstarch,
>   dissolved in 2 tablespoons water
> 1/2-1 teaspoon sesame oil
> Salt to taste, optional

Remove the tough ends of the asparagus and trim the leaf scales from their bottom ends. Wash and drain the spears and cut them on the bias into 1 1/2" lengths.

In a large, heavy skillet or wok, warm the oil over high heat. Add salt and garlic, stirring, until the oil is hot and the garlic sizzles.

Add asparagus and stir for about 1 minute. Add the water, cover the pan, and reduce heat to medium-high. Cook about 2 minutes, or until asparagus are al dente.

Add red pepper and stir for 1 minute or until pepper no longer looks raw.
Stir cornstarch and water mixture, and add it to the pan, stirring constantly until the liquid thickens.
Remove from heat, taste, add salt if desired. Drizzle with sesame oil. Serve hot. Serves 8.

Note: Can be made a few hours ahead, sit at room temperature and be reheated briefly before serving.

Mediterranean Tomato Salad

The distinctive bite of arugula makes this a good choice for an appetizer salad, though it also works well as part of a main course. Arugula may be hard to find in some areas, and when you find it you may be tempted to buy it even if it is no longer really fresh. Don't! Don't spend good money on bad arugula.

8 large ripe tomatoes, cored
Kosher salt and freshly ground black pepper to taste
1 teaspoon sugar
1 large bunch of arugula, washed,
     trimmed and torn into large pieces
1 medium onion, thickly sliced
4 dozen tiny black imported olives,
     or 2 dozen larger ones
4 tablespoons fresh lemon juice
3 tablespoons extra-virgin olive oil, or to taste

Cut tomatoes into wedges. Place them in a shallow bowl and sprinkle them with salt, pepper, and sugar. Cover and set aside for an hour. When ready to serve, arrange a bed of arugula on a platter and spoon tomatoes over it. Strew the onions and olives over the tomatoes.

Mix the lemon juice, olive oil and pepper and drizzle over the salad. Can also be presented in the same way on individual plates. Serve at once. Serves 8.

Broccoli Vinaigrette

1 large clove garlic, minced
1/2 teaspoon salt
1/4 teaspoon freshly ground black pepper
2 tablespoons lemon juice
1/4 cup olive oil
2 pounds broccoli

On a cutting board, sprinkle the salt over the garlic. With the edge and tip of a large knife, mash them together into a purée. Place in a small bowl and add pepper and lemon juice. Gradually whisk in oil.

Trim the broccoli, cut it in spears and steam until just tender. Dress with the vinaigrette. Serve at room temperature. Makes 6-8 servings.

Dill and Green Olive Potato Salad

A favorite company dish, with a twist.

8 medium size potatoes, peeled and cut in eighths
8 green olives cut in quarters
1/4 cup soy mayonnaise
1 small red onion, minced
Pinch of garlic powder
Salt to taste
2 tablespoons of fresh dill

Cook potatoes, drain and cool. Mix in large serving bowl with remaining ingredients. Serves 8.

Variation: 1 medium red bell pepper, lightly sautéed, added or used in place of the olives.

Peach Tart

1/2 cup sugar
1/2 cup margarine, slightly softened
2 cups sifted flour
6 large or 8 medium peaches, peeled,
        quartered and sliced lengthwise
1 tablespoon sugar mixed with 1/2 teaspoon cinnamon
2 or 3 tablespoons currant jelly or apricot jam

Cream margarine and sugar with electric mixer. Add flour and work it in with your hands. Mixture will be crumbly. Spoon it into a 9"x12" pan, and pat it even on the bottom and part way up the sides. Refrigerate 1/2 to 1 hour.

Preheat oven to 350^0 F.
Arrange the peach slices in neat, overlapping rows. Sprinkle generously with cinnamon sugar.

Melt the currant jelly; or if using apricot jam, stir it well. Paint the fruit with the jam or jelly. Bake 30-35 minutes until golden brown. Cut in squares to serve. Serves 8.

Note: Some peaches can easily be peeled with a sharp knife. This is easier to do if you quarter the peaches first. Others need to be dipped in boiling water for 20 or 30 seconds, then in cold water, to loosen their skins.

For a juicier tart, cover the pan with foil; bake 15 minutes, remove foil and finish baking uncovered.

Applesauce Cake

Children will be amazed, and you may be too, when the soda and applesauce react. It's like Chemistry I all over again, but the end results are a lot more fragrant and delicious.

> 1/2 cup margarine
> 1 cup sugar
> 1 teaspoon cinnamon
> 1 teaspoon cloves
> 1 teaspoon nutmeg
> 1 1/2 cups flour
> 1/2 teaspoon salt
> 1/2 cup raisins, optional
> 1 teaspoon baking soda
> 1 cup applesauce

Preheat oven to 375^0 F.
In medium bowl, cream margarine with sugar.
Sift flour, salt, and spices together. If using raisins, put them in a small bowl, remove 1/4 cup of dry mixture and coat raisins with it.

Mix soda with applesauce and add to creamed mixture. Stir in dry ingredients and add raisins, if using.

Bake in greased 9" x 5' x 2" loaf pan for one hour. Serves 6-8.

Creamy Topping

You can make many varieties of delicious sauces and creams from tofu to be used as puddings, substitutes for whipped cream, and for toppings for cakes. The following are standard ones.

1 cup firm tofu
1/4 cup vegetable oil
2 tablespoons honey or sugar
1 tablespoon lemon juice
1 teaspoon vanilla
Dash of salt

Combine all ingredients and blend until smooth. Chill. May need some stirring before serving.

Variation: Substitute for vanilla, 1/2 teaspoon rum flavoring.

Chocolate Cake

A moist rich cake, good on its own or as a basis for your own elaborations.

1 cup sugar
1 1/2 cups flour
1/2 teaspoon salt
1/4 cup cocoa
1 teaspoon soda
1 tablespoon vinegar
1/3 cup vegetable oil
1 teaspoon vanilla
1 cup cold water

Preheat oven to 350^0 F.
Sift first five ingredients into ungreased 8" x 8" baking pan. Add remaining ingredients, and stir gently until smooth. (If you prefer, mix the batter in a bowl.) Bake 35 minutes. Serves 8.

Note: Cake can be doubled and baked in a 9" x 13" pan. Can be split into layers, filled with tofutti and/or topped with strawberries. Or fill and/or frost with chocolate icing. *(Continued for icing)*

Icing:

1 pound box confectioners sugar
1/2 cup margarine, softened
1 teaspoon vanilla extract
3 tablespoons soy milk,
      or 1 1/2 tablespoons each soy milk and water,
      or 3 tablespoons strong coffee
2 squares unsweetened chocolate,
      or 3 1/2 tablespoons unsweetened cocoa

If using cocoa, mix it with the liquid. In a large bowl, beat together margarine, vanilla and liquid. Add sugar gradually until frosting is smooth and spreadable.

If using chocolate baking squares, melt them over very low heat and stir into frosting. Makes enough to fill and frost a 2 layer cake or to frost a 13" x 9" sheet cake.

Israeli Winter Fruit Cup

8 navel oranges
2 juice oranges
4 large bananas
5 moist-dried figs
1 cup raisins
1/2 cup chopped walnuts
2/3 cup sweet red wine
Sugar to taste

Peel and segment the navel oranges, remove all membrane, and chop coarsely. Chop figs. Combine fruits in a large bowl. Slice bananas and add. Squeeze juice from juice oranges and pour over fruit. Stir in raisins, walnuts and wine. add sugar to taste. Serves 8-12.

ROSH HASHANAH

Elul/Tishrei

"There is no approach to revelation other than through creation."
Rabbi Arthur Green, Seek My Face, Speak My Name

Menu 1
Round Challah
Apples Dipped in Sweet Syrup
Israeli Galia Melon Halves with Port
Lentils and Rice
   With Caramelized Onions
Spicy Glazed Carrots
Sweet Potato Apple Bake
Baklava

Menu 2
Round Challah
Apples Dipped in Sweet Syrup
Melon Wedges with Happy Berries
Zucchini Baked
   With Rice and Tomatoes
Green Beans Provencale
Quinoa Salad With Olives
Assorted Cookies

Recipes For Rosh Hashanah At A Glance:
Appetizer: Apples Dipped in Sweet Syrup
Fruits: Israeli Galia Melon Halves With Port, Honeydew Wedges With Happy Berries
Soup: Mushroom and Barley Soup
Entrées: Lentils and Rice With Caramelized Onions, Zucchini Baked With Rice and Tomatoes
Vegetables: Sweet and Spicy Glazed Carrots, Green Beans Provencale, Marinated Plum Tomatoes, Sweet Potato Apple Bake,
Salad: Quinoa Salad With Olives
Desserts: Baklava, Assorted Cookies: Chocolate Peanut Butter Squares, Snowball Cookies, Lace Cookies

At first the Jewish calendar was a solar calendar. At some point in Israel's contact with Babylon the Jewish calendar underwent feminization and became a lunar calendar, its cycle intimate with the female cycle. Unlike the sun, whose shape remains the same throughout the year, the growth and maturation of the moon can be observed. It undergoes change, and change is the visible process of time. During the month, the moon can become a crescent, horns, or a belly of light. The sun is the source of the earth's energy, but the moon is its monthly record of changes and cycles.

The phases of the moon are celebrated in Judaism. *Molad* is the precise time the new moon appears in Jerusalem. *Kiddush Levana* is approximately 14 days, 18 hour and 22 minutes into the lunar cycle, when the new moon has reached its fullest. *Rosh Chodesh*   is the occasion of celebration of the new moon. It has become a special holiday for women.

We begin the Jewish New Year by meditating upon Creation and the Book of Genesis which inscribed the process of creation as blessing. This blessing upon the world, nature, and matter was revolutionary. No more were we to think of nature and matter as evil and hostile to human life, but as the foundation of life without which there can be no spiritual growth. This original blessing for life is the foundation of Judaism from which our values flow, and Genesis is our blueprint for the values of our existence.

One glorious chain of love,
of giving and receiving,
unites all creatures.
None is by or for itself,
but all things exist in continual reciprocal activities--
the One for the all and the all for the One.
None has power, or means for itself;
each receives only in order to give,
and gives in order to receive
and finds therein the purpose of existence.
Rabbi Samson Raphael Hirsch, The Nineteen Letters of Ben Uzziel,

Even in death Jews bless life, for the opposite of life is not death but nothingness, no-life, non-creation, and death is part of the life cycle.

The seed, like the sun and the waters of the earth, is a potent life force. In the writings of the prophets, it is the symbol of the fruitfulness of life, of the blessings of nature and of peace, and is called "the seed of peace."

Yet consider the seed, always small,
sometimes tiny, it contains within it
both the energy to initiate new life and
the wisdom to shape it and direct it.
As its caretakers we can water and enrich the soil it seeks,
and so provide it with surroundings that help it unfold;
but we are not its creators.
The life in it began elsewhere and flows onward,
producing further seed in its turn. It may pass near us---
even through us--- but we are neither its source nor its ultimate destination.
Tiny though it be, a seed is eloquent witness to the Great Life stream,
receiving and transmitting that precious substance.
Rabbi Everett Gendler

"The success of the seed brings peace, because when produce is lacking, jealousy is created among us and that is the cause of hatred and contention. Not so when the crops are plentiful." Metzudath David.

Our first law of kashrut directs us to eat seeds, the potent source of life, and the symbol of peace.

See, I give you every green thing for you to eat,
every seed and herb shall be food for you. (Genesis 1:28-30)

Because we have received and acknowledge life as a blessing, we celebrate the New Year with new fruits and sweet, rich foods, with round foods to symbolize the cycle of the year, and with colorful foods to affirm the blessing of life. Dozens of delicious dishes have become traditional for the Rosh Hashanah meal, such as tsimmis, apple dishes, stuffed dates and figs, fruit pilaf, rice pudding, spinach strudels, chickpeas and couscous, stuffed zucchini, kugel, candied fruits, plum pie.

We bind Rosh Hashanah to Yom Kippur with the custom of dipping challah: on Rosh Hashanah we dip challah in sweet honey, and on Yom Kippur, to break the fast, we dip challah in olive oil spiced with cumin. The poet, Emily Borenstein in her poem "Dipping Bread In Honey," likens the recovery of her father from a terrible illness to the Jewish New Year:

Let one hundred shofar blasts announce your return.
I dip bread in honey to celebrate the New Year.

When the family gathers for the New Year feast, try this Rosh Hashanah quiz for children.

In Genesis, where do the animals live? What is their habitat?
Can you find any cages? or a zoo?
Where does a worm live?
On what day were the animals created?
What were they created from?
On what day were Adam and Eve created?
What were they created from?
What are the names of the trees in the Garden of Eden?
What is the meaning of their names?
When is the last time you looked at the moon?

For centuries, Jewish families have prepared for Rosh Hashanah by cleaning the house from top to bottom. The best cutlery is polished, the finest table linens, china, and crystal are brought out. New clothes for Rosh Hashanah are a long tradition. The whole family would be outfitted with new clothes, including the latest in fall hats.

While immaculate houses and elegant tables still honor the holiday, formality in dress disappeared in the liberating breezes of the 60s and 70s, when parents were pleased if post-adolescent children turned up at all and were grateful if they turned up neat and clean. Many young people became vegetarians during this period, and the trend has persisted, along with a general move towards a lighter and more healthful diet.

Grown children often live too far away now to return for the holidays and senior citizens seek an easier life in the sunbelt. This has given rise to new possible alternatives for enjoying the holidays. We may spend them now with neighbors, friends and colleagues who share the work of planning, shopping and cooking. Many of these groups form their own food traditions and establish menus that persist for years, with each cook contributing a specialty.

Many traditional foods continue to appear, no matter what shape the family or social unit takes. The most familiar symbolic foods for the holiday are the round challahs and the apple dipped in honey. The circular shape of the challah represents infinity, eternity, the New Year wish for a long life. The apple reminds us of the garden of Eden, though scholars believe that the fruit mentioned in the Bible was more likely a pomegranate than an apple; the sweet honey tempers our exile from Eden and conveys the hope for a sweet year ahead. Many other dishes served at the dinner table are also sweetened with honey, carrying out this theme. Though most of us will buy bee honey in a jar from a supermarket, the honey that is cited among the seven sacred species of Israel was not honey from honeycombs, but date honey. Honey from honeycombs probably did not exist in Israel until the era of the Roman occupation. Prior to this period, sweeteners were extracted from grapes, dates and figs.

Sephardic cooks offer foods that imply abundance and fertility by their very profusion: black-eyed peas, pomegranates (for the seeds), sesame seeds, grains of rice and couscous. When cooking the Rosh Hashanah couscous, they leave the lid of the pot slightly ajar to indicate that the year is not yet closed.

The head of the family recites special blessings, all beginning with "Yehi ratzon..." ("May it be Thy will...) over several kinds of vegetables whose names or appearance pun with the good things desired in the coming year. For instance, a gourd stands for fullness, and the head of a fish, a rooster or other animal indicates the hope that all Israel, and each of us individually, will be "the head," and not the tail--that we may go forward, not backward, in the year ahead. This tradition is based on the passage in Deuteronomy 28:13: "...and the Lord will make thee the head, and not the tail." In this cookbook we symbolize that wish in the vegetable world, either by presenting a whole roasted head of garlic, or by using a whole head of beautiful red or green cabbage as part of a centerpiece. You can use all vegetables or a combination of vegetables and fruit, including, for example, a pomegranate, whose myriad seeds are said to equal the 613 commandments we hope to honor in the year ahead.

Apples Dipped in Sweet Syrup

It has been traditional to dip apples in honey, but there are better, healthier alternatives. We suggest brown rice syrup. You might also try maple or corn syrup. For an interesting variation, roll apple slices in coconut flakes, after dipping them in syrup. The best apples for dipping are Cortland apples, because they do not turn color when cut and exposed to air. If you use another variety, toss the slices with a little lemon juice to keep them from oxidizing.

Israeli Galia Melon Halves With Port

What better way to begin the Rosh Hashanah meal than with a fragrant and delicious melon from Israel? Supermarkets sometimes carry them in honor of the holiday, especially if customers create a demand for them. The Ogen or Galia melon are fine Israeli varieties, but if you cannot get them, use what is available.

> 4 Galia melons
> > (or small cantaloupes or other small melons)
>
> 1 cup Port
> Lemon and/or lime wedges for garnish
> Sprigs of mint

Halve and seed melons. Spoon 2 tablespoons Port in each hollow.
Arrange citrus wedges and a mint sprig on each plate alongside melon.
Chill briefly. Melon should not be served icy cold. Serves 8.

Honeydew Wedges with Happy Berries

This is a light and colorful start to an important meal. If you choose to omit the liqueur, use 1 cup of orange juice and a dash of lemon or lime juice.

> 1 very large or 2 small honeydew melons
> 1 cup blueberries, washed
> 1 cup strawberries, hulled, rinsed and halved
> 1/2 cup orange juice
> 1/2 cup orange-flavored liqueur
> Mint sprigs for garnish

Mix berries, juice and liqueur together and allow to macerate. Berries may sit at room temperature up to two hours. If you wish to keep them longer, refrigerate.
Cut melons into halves and seed. Cut into 8 wedges. Arrange on plates with a generous spoonful of drained berries on the side. Garnish with mint sprigs.

Mushroom and Barley Soup

Good for a Rosh Hashanah sit-down dinner.

1 tablespoon oil
1 onion, diced small
1 teaspoon salt
1 bay leaf
1 medium carrot, diced small
1 rib celery diced small and
1 medium potato, diced small
1 cup barley
8 cups water, stock or a mixture of both
3-4 tablespoons fresh dill weed or 1 1/2 teaspoons dried
1 bay leaf
Freshly ground black pepper
1/2 pound mushrooms sliced

Heat oil in a 3 or 4 quart soup pot, sauté onion until soft and clear. Add carrot, celery and potato and cook 5 minutes over medium heat. Add barley, liquid, bay leaf, dill and seasonings. Bring to boil, reduce heat, and simmer partially covered, 1 1/2 to 2 hours, until barley is tender.

Add mushrooms. Simmer 15 more minutes. Garnish with more chopped fresh dill, if desired. Serves 6-8.

Variations: 1. For a rich Old World flavor, add 1/4 cup dried mushrooms with the barley. (Soak the mushrooms in warm water to remove any sand or grit. Rinse well before adding to soup.) 2. Sauté sliced fresh mushrooms briefly before adding to soup.

Lentils and Rice With Caramelized Onions

2/3 cup dried lentils
1 small onion, halved
2 cups water
3 tablespoons oil
3 cups coarsely chopped onions
1 cup long grain rice
2 teaspoons cumin or to taste
1/2 teaspoon salt

44

In a medium saucepan, combine lentils, onion halves, and water. Bring to a boil, lower heat and simmer covered for 15 minutes.

Meanwhile, heat oil and sauté chopped onion in medium skillet over medium-high heat, stirring often, until onions are golden brown. Reduce heat and continue cooking, stirring occasionally until onions are a rich, dark brown, about 30 minutes. Set aside.

Drain lentil cooking liquid into a 2 cup measure. If necessary, add water to equal 2 cups. Discard onion halves. Return liquid to saucepan with rice, cumin, and salt. Stir. Bring to a simmer and cook covered over very low heat until all liquid is absorbed and rice and lentils are tender, about 30 minutes.

Serve topped with caramelized onions. Serves 4-6.

Sweet Potato Apple Bake

This long-time favorite is less sweet than similar dishes.

6 medium sweet potatoes
1 1/2 to 2 cups thinly sliced Cortland apples
Lemon juice (optional, if needed)
1/2 cup brown sugar
3 tablespoons margarine
1/2 cup water or apple-cooking water
Cinnamon

Cook potatoes in boiling water to cover, 30-45 minutes until soft. Drain, cool, and peel them. Cut them into 1/2" thick slices.

Meanwhile, cook apple slices in water barely to cover until almost tender. Drain and save the cooking water. Preheat oven to 350^0 F.

In a greased baking dish, make alternate layers of potatoes and apples, sprinkle with brown sugar, lemon juice if using, and dash of cinnamon; dot with margarine. Pour 1/2 cup reserved apple water over them. Bake uncovered for 1 hour. Serves 6-8.

Zucchini Baked With Rice and Tomatoes

Good company dish. A different way to combine these popular Mediterranean ingredients. Cook rice and onions in advance and assemble the dish at your convenience.

2 pounds zucchini, scrubbed, trimmed, and sliced.
2 cups sliced onions (about 2 medium)
3 medium tomatoes, sliced
1 1/4 cups rice
4 tablespoons olive oil, divided in half
1-2 tablespoons wine vinegar
1-2 cloves garlic, crushed
Salt
Paprika
1/3 cup chopped fresh parsley

Cook rice in boiling water in usual fashion.
In medium saucepan, sauté onions in 2 tablespoons oil until light golden brown.

Preheat oven to 350^0 F.
Oil shallow baking dish. Arrange rice, zucchini, onions and tomatoes in alternate layers, ending with tomatoes on top. Bake 30 minutes or until zucchini slices are tender.

Meanwhile, make a dressing from remaining oil, vinegar, garlic, salt and paprika to taste. When ready to serve, sprinkle casserole with chopped parsley and pour dressing over all. Serves 8-12.

Quinoa Salad With Olives

Quinoa is an Inca grain which has been rediscovered, and is now available in health food stores and specialty markets. Expensive, but a wonderful alternative for a holiday. These tiny grains, about the size of poppy seeds, are an excellent symbol of profusion. They are also healthy, rich in calcium and fiber, and constitute a complete protein. Their pale color is a good foil for the bright and savory vegetables and olives. (If you have never seen cooked quinoa before, you may be surprised by the appearance of the germ rings.)

46

2 cups quinoa
4 cups water
2/3 cup black olives, halved
3/4 cup green olives, halved
1/4 cup pine nuts, lightly toasted
1 bunch scallions, finely chopped
1/4 cup finely chopped fresh parsley
1/2 small red or yellow pepper, cut into thin strips
1 or 2 cloves garlic, minced
2 tablespoons olive oil
2-3 tablespoons white wine vinegar
Salt and pepper

Rinse quinoa well, using a fine strainer. Place quinoa and water in a 2-1/2 quart saucepan, bring to boil. Reduce heat, simmer covered, 10-15 minutes or until water is absorbed. When done, grains will be translucent, and the outer germ ring, which stays opaque, will separate. If water remains in pot when grains are done, stir over low heat until water evaporates.

Allow to cool. Then mix in remaining ingredients, adding vinegar last. Taste and correct seasonings. If making ahead, early in the day or the day before, do not add scallions until ready to serve. Serves 6-8.

Sweet and Spicy Glazed Carrots

Carrots are traditional at Rosh Hashanah, usually served as a tzimmes. Try this recipe for a change.

6 cups sliced carrot rounds (about 2 pounds)
3 tablespoons margarine
1/2 cup brown sugar
3 tablespoons Dijon mustard
1/4 teaspoon salt
2 tablespoons minced parsley

Place carrots and salt in a 2 quart saucepan and cover them with cold water. Bring to the boil, reduce heat, cover and simmer until just tender, about 10-12 minutes. Drain well, and return carrots to the pan. Add margarine, sugar, and mustard and cook, stirring gently, over low heat until carrots are coated with sauce. Taste and adjust flavorings as needed. Garnish with parsley.
Serves 8-12.

Green Beans Provencale

1-1/2 pounds green beans, trimmed
1 cup pitted ripe olives, sliced
2 small cloves garlic, minced
1 teaspoon salt
1/4 cup red wine vinegar
1 teaspoon Dijon mustard
1/2 cup oil, all or part olive oil
2 tablespoons minced fresh parsley
Cherry tomatoes or tomato wedges for garnish

Steam or boil beans until just tender, about 5-8 minutes. Drain and rinse under cold water to keep their color and texture. Remove beans to serving dish, add olives.

In a small bowl, mash garlic and salt, making a paste. Add remaining ingredients. Beat gently with whisk. Pour dressing over beans and olives; toss lightly. Chill until shortly before serving time. Toss again. Garnish with tomatoes. Serves 6-8.

Marinated Plum Tomatoes

Plum tomatoes are a good choice when you long for tomatoes out of season. Of course, they're even better from your garden in season, and often Rosh Hashanah falls when vines are heavy with tomatoes.

8 plum tomatoes
8 cloves garlic, quartered
1/2 cup chopped fresh basil
1 1/2 tablespoons olive oil
Salt and freshly ground pepper to taste

Cut tomatoes in half lengthwise, then into small wedges. Add remaining ingredients, and mix well. Cover. Marinate for 2 hours. Serves 6-8.

Baklava

A great holiday dessert for any holiday, except Pesach.

Light syrup: to be made day before
1 cup sugar
2 cups water
Juice from 1 lemon

In a saucepan, melt sugar in water with lemon juice over medium heat.
Bring to boil, then simmer until liquid forms a light syrup, about 20 minutes.
Remove from heat and cool.

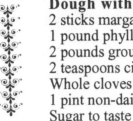

Dough with filling:
2 sticks margarine, melted
1 pound phyllo pastry dough
2 pounds ground walnut meats
2 teaspoons cinnamon
Whole cloves for garnish
1 pint non-dairy whipped topping, optional
Sugar to taste

Preheat oven to 350⁰ F.
Grease large cookie tray with melted margarine.
Lay down 1 sheet phyllo dough in pan; brush surface generously with margarine. Cover with second sheet. Repeat until 1/3 of phyllo leaves are used.

Mix walnuts and cinnamon. Spread half of walnut cinnamon mixture evenly over phyllo layers. Sprinkle with sugar. Build up another layer of phyllo, using a third of phyllo leaves and repeat with walnuts, cinnamon and sugar. Use remaining phyllo leaves to make a third layer. Brush top layer generously with margarine.

Cut into diagonal stripes, 2" wide, across the pan. Cut intersecting diagonals to make diamonds. Insert clove in each diamond. Bake about 30 minutes or until top layer of phyllo dough is brown and shiny.

Remove from oven, drain excess margarine by tilting pan. Immediately pour the cold syrup over the hot baklava. Tilt pan again until syrup coats each diamond lightly. If surface is not shiny, brush diamonds with leftover margarine to give it luster. Serve with non-dairy cream, if desired. Serves 12.

Chocolate Peanut Butter Squares

Much as we loved the dear tantes who made the jawbreaking taiglach we dreaded on Rosh Hashanah, these have a greater appeal to children and to one's inner child.

> 2 cups peanut butter, divided
> 3/4 cup margarine, softened
> 2 cups powdered sugar
> 3 cups graham cracker crumbs, about 36 crackers
> 2 cups (12 oz. package) semi-sweet chocolate chips,
> divided in half

In large mixer bowl, beat together 1 1/4 cups peanut butter and margarine until well-blended and creamy. Gradually beat in half the powdered sugar. Turn off beaters and use hands or a spoon to incorporate the remaining sugar, the graham cracker crumbs, and 1/2 cup chips.

Lightly grease a 13" x 9" baking pan and press the mixture evenly into it. Use a spatula to smooth the top.

Melt remaining chocolate with remaining peanut butter in a medium-size, heavy bottomed saucepan over very low heat. Stir constantly until smooth. Spoon over graham cracker base, making a thick, even layer of frosting. Chill one hour or longer, till chocolate is firm. Cut into bars; keep covered in fridge. Makes about 60.

Snow Ball Cookies

Children love to shape these cookies and cover them with "snow." It's a good way to have them participate in the holiday preparation.

> 1 cup shortening
> 2 cups flour
> 1/4 cup sugar
> 1/2 teaspoon salt
> 1 cup walnuts, chopped
> 2 teaspoons vanilla
> Confectioners' sugar

In large bowl, cut shortening into flour, using a pastry blender or two knives. When mixture resembles coarse meal, add sugar and salt, then nuts and vanilla. Use hands to press into a cohesive mass.

Preheat oven to 350^0 F. Shape dough into 1 1/4" balls, place on ungreased baking sheets. Bake 15-17 minutes. Remove to cooling racks. Use a strainer to sift powdered sugar over cookies while hot. Makes about 2 1/2 dozen cookies.

Lace Cookies

A sophisticated, delicate, melt-in-the--mouth cookie.

1/3 cup margarine, softened
2/3 cup firmly-packed brown sugar
1/4 teaspoon salt
1/2 teaspoon baking powder
1 cup oatmeal, uncooked (quick or regular)
1/2 cup chopped nuts
1 tablespoon soy milk
1 teaspoon vanilla

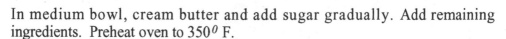

In medium bowl, cream butter and add sugar gradually. Add remaining ingredients. Preheat oven to 350^0 F.

Drop by teaspoonfuls onto ungreased cookie sheets. Leave about 2" between cookies to allow room to spread. Bake about 8 minutes, or until cookies are a golden brown. Watch carefully for last few minutes of baking, to make sure they don't burn.

Remove from oven, cool 2-3 minutes before removing from cookie sheets. (Use a wide metal spatula) Makes about 2 1/2 dozen.

YOM KIPPUR

Tishrei/Cheshvan

It is necessary to feed one's animals, even on Yom Kippur, for we must have compassion on the animals so that heaven will have compassion on us.
Joseph ben Moses

Menu 1:
Erev Yom Kippur
Challah Dipped in Olive Oil
Mock Chopped Liver and Crackers
Artichokes and Lemon Sauce
Spaghetti Casserole With Zucchini
Simple Slaw
Molasses Orange Bread

Menu 2:
Leil Yom Kippur--After The Fast
Almond Milk, or
Challah Dipped in Olive Oil
Spiced Chickpeas and Rice,
or Eggplant Etzleinu
Mixed Green Salad
Chocolate Tofu Pie

Recipes for Yom Kippur At A Glance:
Breaking Fast: Challah Dipped in Olive Oil, Almond Milk
Appetizers: Mock Chopped Liver, Artichokes In Lemon Sauce
Entrées: Spiced Chickpeas and Rice, Eggplant Etzleinu, Spaghetti Casserole with Zucchini, Sesame Orzo Pasta, Rotini and Vegetable Bake
Salads: Tomatoes With Vidalia Onions, Simple Cole Slaw, Couscous Salad
Desserts: Molasses Orange Bread, Chocolate Tofu Pie

There is an old tradition that Jews do not wear leather on Yom Kippur, so that violence to animals will not be counted against us. We should not eat meat for the same reason.

The Yom Kippur fast requires careful handling for a healthy fast. Begin and break your fast gently with holiday challah, wine, apples, honey, fruits, and a vegetarian meal. It is a mistake to think that eating a heavy meal the night before a fast will carry you easily through the next day. On the contrary, the body works very hard if it is overloaded with heavy food immediately prior to fasting.

Dr. Elliot Berry, head of clinical nutrition at Hebrew University-Hadassah Medical School, recommends frequent drinks of water throughout the day before the fast begins, and suggests that the last meal should include complex carbohydrates: foods like macaroni, rice, potatoes and whole-grain bread. "When complex carbohydrates are stored in the liver, water is retained and the body suffers less dehydration during the fast." He also advises against salty or sweet foods and carbonated beverages before the fast, since they make you thirsty. Do not to drink too much alcohol or caffeine. (This diet is also recommended when flying to avoid or mitigate jet lag.)

Professor Ya'acov Bar-Tana, head of the Medical Biochemistry Department at Hebrew University, also advises against overeating the night before the fast, and suggests that the fast should be broken first by drinking liquids, but definitely not carbonated beverages, and by eating a slice of bread or dry cake one hour before the meal. Dipping a slice of challah into olive oil, with a gentle herb in it, is a delicious and healthy way to break the fast. Try putting minced pieces of roasted garlic into the oil, or a sprinkle of tarragon.

Fasting should make us sensitive to those who fast involuntarily, the victims of famine and malnutrition. We struggle to control our hunger pangs for one day. There are those who live out their lives in this struggle. They are born into famine and die in famine. Pity the mother whose baby dies of diarrhea and dehydration because of the lack of a bottle of water with a little glucose in it. Pity the child born into this world who has never had its hunger satisfied. We break our fast with joy. Others never break their fast.

Parpisa

Parpisa, a tradition among Mediterranean Jews is a ceremony similar to *shlogen kapores* , the Ashkenazic ritual in which a living chicken is swung around one's head in a symbolic enactment that one's sins are transferred to the chicken. Parpisa is more humane and more appropriate to a season that celebrates the creation of the world. As Shalom Spiegel describes it in his book about the Akedah, *The Last Trial,* about fifteen or twenty days before Rosh ha-Shanah, weave a basket for each child of the household "and fill it with earth and manure; plant in the baskets seeds of wheat, barley, and Egyptian peas or various kinds of beans....The seeds grow about one or two handbreadths high." You need not weave the baskets, but you should plant the seeds in them, choosing seeds that are available or relevant to your region. Each child takes a basket and swings it round his head seven times and recites: "This instead of me, this is my proxy, this is my substitute--and casts it into the river.'" (p. 119)

Almond Milk

There are many recipes for nut milks, which are both ancient and modern. Almond milk is a wonderful old substitute for dairy, before dairy products became popular in the last two centuries. It was in fact one of the earliest drinks known to the human race. Middle Eastern Jews still use it in a variety of recipes. Iraqi Jews break the Yom Kippur fast with an almond milk drink. Persian Jews mix it with rosewater; Lebanese Jews mix it with apricots. There are many varieties of almond milk drinks, and if beaten until thick can be used as a cream sauce. There are many ways to make almond milk; the following is a simple recipe:

Easy Almond Nut Milk

1/2 cup almonds
1 1/2 cups boiling water

Blend almonds and boiling water together for about 3 minutes at high speed. Strain through muslin or cheesecloth. (The remaining pulp can be used in vegetable/nut loaves.) Shake milk before using. Makes about 1 1/2 cups.

Olive Oil for Dipping

2 cups olive oil, or enough for guests
8-12 cloves garlic (may be roasted beforehand)
2 red peppers, deribbed, cut in 2" chunks
(may be roasted beforehand, or steamed for about 2-3 minutes)

Moc Chopped Liver

Incredibly delicious and sure to be a favorite for other holidays as well. Can be prepared the day before.

1/2 package (1 cup) brown lentils
1 large diced onion
1 cup chopped walnuts
Salt to taste

Put lentils in a 2 or 3 quart pot, and cover with water. Use water sparingly so that lentils absorb all the water. More water can be added as needed. Bring water to a boil, partially cover and simmer for about 45 minutes. Check occasionally to make sure water has not boiled off, and add water as needed.

Sauté onions until lightly golden and tender.
Purée lentils in food processor. Purée walnuts until slightly coarse. Mix all ingredients together. Salt to taste. Chill about 2 hours. Serve with crackers or rye bread, or on lettuce leaves.

Artichokes in Lemon Sauce

A welcome light vegetable dish to follow the fast.

6 artichokes, fresh or canned
grated rind from 2 lemons
2 quarts cold water
1 defrosted, drained 12 ounce bag of frozen mixed
        vegetables (peas, carrots, beans and corn)

Fill a 2 quart saucepan with water, put lemon rinds in the water, and set aside. Peel and clean the outer leaves of the artichokes. Core out the centers. Put stems into the acidulated water with the artichoke hearts, to prevent them from turning black. *(Continued)*

Sauce:
Juice of two lemons
2 teaspoons of sugar
1/4 cup olive oil
2 cups water
Salt and pepper to taste
Chopped fresh dill (optional)

Put all ingredients into a saucepan and bring to a roiling boil, turn heat to low. Place artichokes with hearts down in the middle of the pot. Arrange drained, mixed vegetables around artichokes. Sprinkle salt, pepper and dill. Cover, simmer gently for about 30 minutes, or until artichokes are tender. Do not overcook, or artichokes will get mushy.

Spiced Chickpeas and Rice

1 cup uncooked chickpeas,
        or two large cans of prepared chickpeas, drained
3 cups water, if using dried chickpeas
1 tablespoon oil
1 large onion, minced
1 large green pepper, diced
1 large tomato, cubed
1/2 teaspoon salt
1 1/2 teaspoons cumin, or to taste
1 8 ounce can of tomato sauce
1 cup brown rice
2 cups water for rice

The night before, soak chickpeas in water. In the morning, bring water to boil, and let simmer 3-4 hours in large pot partially covered, or use 2 cans of prepared, drained chickpeas.

Cook brown rice in water. While rice is cooking, sauté onion in small amount of oil in large skillet. When oil is absorbed, add small amounts of water until onion is translucent and tender. Add green pepper, cook 5 minutes. Add tomato, cook another 5 minutes. Add tomato sauce. Drain chickpeas and add to skillet. Add salt and cumin, cover and simmer for about five minutes. Serve over rice. Serves 6-8.

Variations: Dish can be varied according to taste, with red pepper instead of green pepper, or by substituting a tablespoon of chili powder for the cumin.

Eggplant Etzleinu

On Yom Kippur we often need dishes that will feed our many friends we break the fast with. This is a good company dish that is rich and filling.

Plan Ahead Tip: Make the vegetable mixture a day in advance.

      1 eggplant, about 1 1/2 pounds
Coarse kosher salt
3 or 4 tablespoons olive oil
1 medium onion, chopped
1 rib celery, chopped
1 clove garlic, minced
1 teaspoon salt
1/4 teaspoon freshly ground black pepper
1/2 teaspoon each basil and oregano, crumbled
2 tablespoons red wine
2 tablespoons tomato paste
2 8 ounce cans tomato sauce
1 pound penne,
    cooked according to package directions, drained
1 green pepper, seeded, deribbed and chopped
1/2 pounds fresh mushrooms, cut in thirds
1 tablespoon minced parsley
1-2 tablespoons bread crumbs

Cut off the eggplant cap, but leave the skin on. Make 1/2 " thick slices, then cut across to make 1/2" cubes. Place the eggplant in a colander and salt it liberally. Place a plate on top of the eggplant and weight it with a large can or other heavy object. After half an hour, rinse off the eggplant, and gently squeeze it dry in a clean towel,

In a large Dutch oven or 12" skillet, heat the oil and add eggplant, onions, and celery. Sauté until the onion is translucent and the eggplant is lightly browned. Add the garlic and sauté one minute. Add salt, pepper, basil, oregano, red wine and tomato paste and sauce. Stir, bring to a boil, reduce heat, cover; simmer over low heat for 10 minutes. Add green pepper, mushrooms, and parsley and simmer another 5 minutes.

Preheat oven to 350^0 F.
Oil a 3 quart casserole or deep baking dish and place a layer of 1/3 of the pasta. Cover with a third of the eggplant mixture and repeat twice, making six alternating layers in all, ending with vegetables. Sprinkle with breadcrumbs. Bake uncovered 20 minutes. Serves 6-8.   *(Continued)*

Note: If eggplant mixture seems dry, add a little water to it before assembling the casserole. Depending on the size and shape of the baking dish, you may not use all of the pasta. Any extra will keep a day or two until you are read to use it in another preparation.

Spaghetti Casserole with Zucchini

> 1/2 pound spaghetti
> 2 cups grated zucchini
> 1/2 teaspoon salt or to taste
> Margarine for dotting
> 1/2 cup wheat germ
> Paprika

Grate zucchini, put into colander, sprinkle with salt and drain for 15 minutes. Press remaining water from zucchini.

Meantime, cook spaghetti. Preheat oven to 350^0 F. When spaghetti is cooked, drain, mix well with zucchini. Add salt to taste. Grease a 7" x 11" oven casserole. Put spaghetti and zucchini mixture into casserole. Sprinkle with wheat germ, dot with margarine. Sprinkle with paprika. Bake 20 minutes. Serves 6 as a side dish, or 4 as an entrée.

Sesame Orzo Pasta

> 1/2 box orzo (1/2 pound)
> cooked according to directions, drained
> 1 tablespoon vegetable oil
> 1/2 pound fresh green beans, cut in 2" lengths
> 1 large red pepper, or two small red peppers,
> cut into 2" lengths
> 1/8-1/4 cup sesame oil
> 1/4 cup pignoli nuts (optional)

Lightly sauté green beans and red peppers in 1 tablespoon light vegetable oil in a large skillet. Add to drained orzo. Add amount of sesame oil, to taste. Mix well. Chill in serving bowl one hour. Just before serving, mix in pignoli nuts. Serves 6-8.

Rotini and Vegetable Bake

4 tablespoons olive oil
4 tablespoons margarine
4-6 cloves garlic, crushed
1/4 cup chopped parsley
1/2 teaspoon dried oregano
1 teaspoon dried basil
4 ounce can mushroom caps with liquid
1 package (10 ounces) frozen cauliflower florets,
                    thawed
1 package (10 ounces) frozen broccoli florets, thawed
1 pound box rotini
1/2 teaspoon salt
Black pepper to taste
6 ounce can small pitted black olives and 1/2 its liquid

Topping:
1/4-1/3 cup bread crumbs
2 tablespoons margarine, melted
Salt, pepper, and garlic powder to taste

Preheat oven to 350⁰ F.
Heat margarine and oil in 12" skillet or wok. Sauté garlic, herbs, and mushrooms. Add broccoli and cauliflower and sauté gently for about 5 minutes.

Cook rotini according to package directions. Drain pasta and add gradually to skillet with olives, turning gently to mix with sauce. Add salt and pepper. Spoon into a lightly oiled 9 x 13 baking pan or large casserole. Mix topping ingredients and scatter over top. Bake covered for 15 minutes. Uncover and bake 15 minutes more. Serves 6-8.

Cabbage, Apple, and Nut Salad

1/2 medium head of cabbage, shredded
2 apples, cored and diced
1 cup chopped walnuts
1/2 cup raisins (optional)
2 tablespoons soy mayonnaise (or to taste)

Toss ingredients lightly altogether. Chill. Serves 4-6

Tomatoes with Vidalia Onions and Balsamic Vinegar

In its simplicity, this mouth-watering salad demonstrates the principle of "less is more." It also shows how today's market responds to the needs of up-to-date kosher consumers. When balsamic vinegar first became popular in the U.S. a few years ago, no kosher brand existed. Today there are several.

6-8 medium tomatoes, cut in wedges, then halved
1 medium Vidalia onion, quartered and thinly sliced
1 tablespoon balsamic vinegar
1 or 2 pinches sugar

In a serving bowl, mix the onions and tomatoes gently. Sprinkle with the vinegar and sugar. Serve at room temperature, or slightly chilled.

Note: If Vidalia onions are unavailable, use another mild, sweet variety, such as Spanish or Bermuda.

Simple Cole Slaw

Crisp, light, delicious. The dill makes all the difference.

1 1/2 pound cabbage
2 carrots
1/4-1/2 cup chopped fresh dill

Dressing:
3/4 cup soy mayonnaise
1/3-1/2 cup red wine vinegar
1 tablespoon Dijon or dark mustard
1 tablespoon sugar
Salt and freshly ground black pepper to taste

Trim and core cabbage, cut into wedges, then into 2" chunks. Chop in processor with steel blade in place, 2 cups at a time, using 2-5 pulses per batch. Remove to large bowl. Makes about 8 cups. Change to shredding disk to grate carrots. Add to cabbage, along with the dill, mix well.

In a small bowl, whisk together soy mayonnaise, vinegar, mustard and sugar. Taste and adjust flavors to your palate. Add salt and pepper to taste. Pour over slaw, mix thoroughly. Refrigerate 1-2 hours before serving. Keeps about 5 days. Makes about 10 servings.

Couscous Salad

    1 cup couscous
    1 1/3 cups water
    5 tablespoons olive or vegetable oil
    2 tablespoons lime juice
    1 1/2 tablespoons wine vinegar
    1/2 teaspoon salt
    1/4 teaspoon pepper
    1/2 cup finely chopped radishes (about 4 or 5 whole)
    1/2 cup finely chopped celery
    1/3 cup chopped, seeded cucumber
               (about 1/2 small cuke)
    1/4 cup thinly sliced scallions
    1/4 cup chopped fresh parsley
    1/4 cup chopped fresh mint (optional, but delicious)

In small saucepan, bring water to boil. Place couscous in large bowl and pour water over it. Cover with plate. Allow to stand 5 minutes.

Combine oil, lime juice, vinegar, salt and pepper in a small screwtop jar. Cover and shake well. Drizzle 3 tablespoons dressing over couscous. Let stand another 5 minutes. Fluff mixture lightly with fork. Cool.

Add vegetables and herbs, toss with remaining dressing. Cover and chill until about 30 minutes before serving time. Serve at room temperature. Serves 6.

Molasses-Orange Bread

Is it a bread or is it a cake? It tastes like the best honey cake there ever was.

    1/2 cup sugar
    2 2/3 cups sifted all-purpose flour
    2 teaspoons baking powder
    1/2 teaspoon baking soda
    1 1/2 teaspoons salt
    1 cup coarsely chopped nuts or raisins
    2/3 cup soy milk
    1 tablespoon grated orange rind
    1/2 cup orange juice
    2 tablespoons vegetable oil
    1/2 cup molasses

Preheat oven to 325⁰ F.

In a large bowl, sift sugar, flour, baking soda, baking powder and salt. Add nuts or raisins. Combine remaining ingredients and add to flour mixture all at once, stirring just enough to blend.

Bake in a well-greased loaf pan, about 9"x 5"x 2-3/4", for 75 minutes. Cool before removing from pan.

Note: Can be frozen, but will lose the orange flavor.

Chocolate Tofu Pie

This recipe gets raves--and deserves them. You can feed it to children --and others--who won't eat tofu in any other form. It's also easy to make and healthy.

Graham Cracker Crust:
1 1/2 cups graham cracker crumbs
1/4 cup (1/2 stick) margarine, cut in small pieces

Filling:
1 cup semi-sweet chocolate chips
2 tablespoons water
1 pound soft or silken tofu
1/4 cup soy milk
1/3 cup honey
1 teaspoon vanilla extract

Preheat oven to 350⁰ F.

Grind graham crackers thoroughly in food processor. Add margarine and continue processing until it is well combined with the crumbs. Press mixture in the bottom and sides of a 9" pie pan.

In a heavy-bottomed saucepan or in the top of a double boiler, melt chocolate chips with 2 tablespoons water.

Wash and dry the work bowl of the food processor. Put tofu and melted chocolate in it and process until perfectly smooth. Stir in remaining ingredients. Pour filling into the crust and bake 30-35 minutes, until filling is firm and crust is golden. May be served at room temperature or chilled. Serves 6-8. Best made a day ahead.

SUKKOT

Tishrei

Menu 1
Butternut Squash Bisque
Bean and Corn Tamale Pie
Zucchini Salad
Chocolate Cake

Menu 2
Many Hands Casserole
Superior Succotash
Carrot Salad
Molasses Cranberry Pudding

Menu 3
Polenta With Leek and Mushroom Topping
Stuffed Acorn Squash
Lemony Green Beans
Cranberry Nut Bars

Recipes for Sukkot At A Glance:
Bread: *Corn Bread*
Soups: *Butternut Squash Bisque, Fava Bean soup*
Entrées: *Superior Sukkotash, Stuffed Acorn Squash, Many-Hands Winter Casserole, Many-Hands Summer Casserole, Polenta With Leek and Mushroom Topping*
Side Dish : *Molasses Cranberry Pudding*
Salads: *Carrot Salad, Zucchini Salad, Lemon Lover's Green Beans*
Dessert: *Cranberry Nut Bars*

On the first day you shall take the product of citron trees, branches of palm trees, boughs of leafy trees, and willows of the brook, and you shall rejoice before the Lord your God seven days....You shall live in booths seven days in order that future generations shall know that I made the Israelite people live in booths when I brought them out of the land of Egypt. (Lev. 23:40)

Sukkot is also known as The Feast of Tabernacles, the Feast of Booths and the Feast of the Ingathering. The holiday begins on the night of the full moon of the autumnal equinox. Because it marks the fall harvest festival, the final harvest of the year in Israel, we decorate the sukkah with fruits and vegetables to commemorate the way the early Israelites lived in booths with open thatched roofs during this harvest time. This is a wonderful holiday for children to participate in. Let children help build and decorate the sukkah.

If you have the land, you can build one in your backyard. If not, you can create one on an apartment balcony or build a community sukkah at a temple or synagogue. There are even sukkah kits available for sukkahs to be put up like a tent that can easily be taken down. The *Jewish Catalogue* (I, p.129-130) gives information on how to build a sukkah, and cautions that "The sukkah should not be an elegant structure. A rough shack built by hand is the ideal." The sukkah is not intended to be a permanent structure. Its beauty comes from the decorations inside, the company, the songs and the food.

Four species symbolize the fertility and joy of the harvest: the etrog, and the palm lulav, the myrtle and the willow, whose branches are bound together in a wand collectively called the lulav. In temple we bless them every day of the holiday, and carry them in a procession around the sanctuary.

The blessing for the lulav is:

Blessed art Thou, Lord our God, Creator of the World,
Who has commanded us concerning the taking up of the lulav.

On the eighth day of Sukkot, Shemini Atzeret, the Eighth Day of Solemn Assembly, a prayer for rain is introduced into the daily Musaf service. This is the beginning of the rainy season in Israel, a time of concern, for the rains are essential for the coming year's harvest. The following is a portion of this prayer.

Remember Aaron the priest and his ritual immersions in water.
On Yom Kippur he kept the rites with water;
He read from the Torah and bathed himself in water.

For Aaron's sake, do not withhold water.

Remember Israel's tribes; You brought them through water.
For their sake brackish marsh became sweet water;
Their descendants' blood was spilled for You like water.

For the people Israel's sake, grant the gift of water.

You are the Lord our God
Who causes the wind to blow and the rain to fall

The prayer for rain is paralleled by a prayer for dew recited on the first day of Hag ha Matzot, anchoring our reflections on our dependence upon nature and God's mercy.

Other appropriate readings for Sukkot are:

"...it is good, yea, it is comely for us to eat and to drink and to enjoy pleasure for all our labor, wherein we have labored under the sun, all the days of our lives which God has given us; for this is our portion. Each of us to whom God has given such riches and wealth, and has given us the power to eat and to take our portion, and to rejoice in our labor--this is the gift of God."
Ecclesiastes Ch. 5, v. 17-18

"A feast is made for laughter, and wine maketh glad the life."
Ch. 10, v. 19

On Shabbat in the middle of Sukkot, we read history from Exodus, prophecy from Ezekiel, and the wise and moody poetry and prose of Ecclesiastes. The quotes above, from the book's sunnier moments, sum up the spirit of the harvest feast. The second quote is equally appropriate on Simchat Torah.

Though we don't live in a sukkah for seven days, we should try to eat some meals there if we can, and make them full of all the best of our local harvest. Stuffed foods, as symbols of abundance, are traditional on Sukkot. Try the ones given here, or check the index for others.

Cornbread

This bread has an intense corn flavor which makes it a natural dish for this season. It is also delicious for breakfast spread with orange marmalade.

1 cup cornmeal
1 cup flour
1/4 cup sugar
5 teaspoons baking powder
1/2 teaspoon salt
1 cup plus 2 tablespoons water
1/3 cup oil

Preheat oven to 425^0 F. Grease and flour an 8" X 8" pan. In a medium bowl, stir dry ingredients together. Add liquids, and stir to combine thoroughly. Bake in prepared pan about 20-25 minutes. Serves 8-10.

Butternut Squash Bisque

A stand-out in flavor and nutrition, this aromatic soup is well-suited for any fall or winter holiday (but can be enjoyed in the summer too).

2 teaspoons unsalted margarine
2 large carrots, peeled and sliced
1 cup chopped onion
1 clove garlic, minced
1 tablespoon minced fresh ginger
2 teaspoons curry powder
1/4 teaspoon ground cinnamon
1/8 teaspoon ground nutmeg
2 medium butternut squash,
     about 2 pounds each, peeled, seeded
     and cut into chunks
3 cups apple juice

Melt margarine in a 3 quart saucepan over medium heat. Add carrots, onion and garlic. Cook over medium-high heat until tender, about 5 minutes. Add ginger, curry, cinnamon and nutmeg. Cook for 1 minute. Add squash and apple juice. Heat to a boil. Cover, reduce heat and simmer for 15 minutes or until squash is tender.

Purée soup in several batches in blender or processor until smooth. Reheat. May be served hot or chilled. Serves 6-8.

Note: If a thinner soup is desired, add water, a little at a time, to reach desired consistency.

Fava Bean Soup

This soup was mentioned in cookbooks from Marseilles and Alsace as a dish for Sukkot. It calls for few ingredients and is easy to make because there is no chopping. However you will have to spend time removing the skins from the beans. Children might enjoy doing this, and it might be a good way to engage with them in "quality" time.

The fava bean is ancient and is also known as broad bean, or in Hebrew and Arabic as *ful*. It is still a popular food in the Middle East and North Africa. Jews who came to France from Algeria and Morocco in the 1960s brought this soup with them.

> 1 pound dried fava beans
> 1 tablespoon olive oil
> 2 cloves garlic, peeled
> 1 teaspoon cumin, or to taste
> 1 teaspoon harissa
> 1 bay leaf
> Freshly ground black pepper to taste
> 2 quarts water
> 2 teaspoons salt, or to taste

Soak beans overnight in water to cover. They will double in volume. Drain and rinse beans. Pinch each bean between thumb and forefinger to pop off the heavy outer skin.

In a 3 or 4 quart pot, warm the oil. Add the garlic, cumin, and harissa, and cook one minute. add the beans, bay leaf, pepper and water. Bring to the boil, reduce heat, and simmer, partially covered, 2 1/2 hours or until beans are tender. (This could vary greatly with age and origin of beans.) Remove bay leaf. Add salt to taste. If you wish, mash the beans in the pot with a potato masher, or purée some of the soup in a blender or food processor and reheat. Serves 8.

Note: Harissa is a Middle Eastern condiment--very hot. If unavailable, substitute hot sauce to taste.

Superior Succotash

Mellow flavors, textures and a kaleidoscope of luscious garden colors make this a perfect dish for a harvest feast.

2 cups fresh or frozen baby lima beans
4 tablespoons oil
3 cups finely chopped red onion
1 teaspoon minced garlic
4 tomatoes in 1/2" dice
Salt and freshly ground black pepper to taste
1/4 cup minced parsley
3 cups fresh corn kernels off the cob
      or 3 cups frozen corn kernels

Cook fresh beans in boiling water to cover, about 10 minutes or until tender. Cook frozen beans according to package directions. Drain beans.
In large skillet, heat oil, add onion. Sauté gently until wilted, stirring often.

Add garlic and cook a minute or two. Add tomatoes, salt, pepper, and parsley. Cook another minute. Add corn and beans, cook 2 more minutes. Serves 8.

Stuffed Acorn Squash

Created by Gloria Bakst, the ingredients show off traditional harvest produce.

6 small size acorn squash
 2 cups fresh or frozen cranberries
1/2 cup raisins
1 cup water
1/4 cup chopped walnuts
4 large apples (Macintosh or Cortland),
      peeled and chopped fine
2 cups cooked basmati or brown rice
1 tablespoon brown rice syrup
Apple juice as needed

Simmer raisins in water for 20 minutes. Do not drain. Mix together all remaining ingredients, except squash. Add the raisins and water. If mixture seems dry, add apple juice to moisten.

Preheat oven to 350⁰ F.

Cut tops off squash and trim bottoms so squash sits flat. Fill squash as full as possible, packing tightly. Arrange in shallow, oven-proof dish, and bake 1 hour, or until squash is tender. Bake any extra filling in a separate dish for 25 minutes. Serves 6.

Notes: Choose 6 squash that are small enough for individual portions, or choose 3 larger ones and serve a half squash per person. To bake squash in microwave: arrange squash in microwave dish. Cover with wax paper. Cook on high for 30 minutes. Cook extra stuffing separately for 5 minutes on high.

Many Hands Winter Casserole

This is a dish that grew and changed as it passed from Irma Natan's daughter-in-law to Irma to us. It can be made with almost any combination of vegetables. Cook it slowly about 1 1/2 hours at 325⁰ F. Make enough for the next day. It tastes even better after the flavor sets a while, and can be served over pasta, if desired.

1 large onion, sliced
3 medium potatoes, cut in 2" chunks
2 medium sweet potatoes, cut in 2" chunks
2 carrots, cut in thick strips
1 large red pepper, seeded, deribbed,
            and cut in 3" strips
1 medium eggplant, peeled, cut in 2" chunks
1/2 pound mushrooms, halved
Salt and freshly ground pepper to taste
1/4 cup olive oil
4 cloves of garlic in large dice

Preheat oven to 325⁰ F.

Cover bottom of heavy casserole or Dutch oven with layer of olive oil. Make layers of vegetables in order given. Sprinkle each layer with salt and pepper to taste. Scatter diced garlic over last layer of vegetables. Drizzle remainder of olive oil over all. Bake covered about 1 1/2 hours. Add water as necessary during baking to keep vegetables moist.

Serve as is with pita or French bread, or over pasta or rice. Serves 8-10.

(Continued)

Variations:
1 large green pepper instead of red pepper
2 scrubbed zucchini, cut into 2" rounds
1/2 teaspoon tarragon sprinkled over the top
1/2 teaspoon chili powder for a snappy taste

For a lighter dish, omit olive oil on top. Instead, mix 2 tablespoons tomato paste with 1 cup water and pour over vegetables.

Whatever variation you choose, check the level of moisture from time to time. If the vegetables are cooking too fast and loosing moisture, add water to cover the bottom of the casserole.

Many-Hands Summer Casserole

A stove top version of previous recipe, which is a vegetable stew. Good for hot weather, because oven does not have to be lit.

2 large onions, sliced
1 tablespoon olive oil, or spray
4-6 medium size potatoes, quartered
2 seeded, green peppers, cut in 2" chunks
2 large carrots, cut in 2" chunks
1/2 pound mushrooms, left whole
2 tomatoes, cut in chunks
1 (8 ounce) can tomato sauce
2-3 drops of Chinese hot oil, optional
2-3 fresh bay leaves

Oil or spray a large Dutch oven.
Sauté onions until translucent. Add vegetables in layers. Add seasoning. Pour tomato sauce over the top. Cover and cook on low heat for 1 hour. Check moisture. Add water, if necessary. Serves 6-8; more if served over rice.

Molasses Cranberry Pudding

                3 cups all-purpose flour
                1/2 cup sugar
                2 teaspoons baking powder
                1/2 teaspoon salt
                2 teaspoons cinnamon
                1/2 teaspoon ginger
                2 1/2 cups cranberries, chopped in processor
                1 cup molasses
                2/3 cup warm water
                1/4 cup melted margarine

Preheat oven to 350^0 F.
In a large bowl, sift together flour, sugar, baking powder, salt and spices.
Stir in cranberries. Combine molasses, water and margarine; stir into flour.
Turn into greased 9" x 13" pan. Bake 30 minutes. Serves 12.

Note: Recipe may be halved and baked in an 8" square pan 20-25 minutes.

Carrot Salad

In the early decades of this century, East European Jewish immigrants spent only 10% of their food budget on fruits and vegetables. Jewish home economists deplored this diet as too rich, too highly seasoned, and not properly balanced. The experts of those days would be pleased by the new emphasis on vegetables, but this Moroccan-inspired dressing might be too bold for them.

People who avoid black foods during the holiday for symbolic reasons may substitute green olives or omit them altogether. This bright and beautiful salad can stand on its own.

                1/3 cup vegetable or olive oil
                2 tablespoons lemon juice
                2 cloves garlic, minced
                1 pound carrots, grated or shredded
                3 tablespoons minced parsley
                Salt and pepper to taste
                1/4 teaspoon sugar
                        (optional, depending on sweetness of carrots)
                Black olives (optional garnish)

In large bowl, mix oil and lemon juice, parsley and garlic. Add carrots and toss gently. Season with salt and pepper and, if desired, sugar.
Chill. Can be made a day ahead. Garnish with olives, if desired. Serves 6-8.

Zucchini Salad

There are two schools of thought about cooking zucchini. One school finds it bland and in need of elaborate seasoning, and the other thinks it needs only a simple sauté and a little salt and pepper. This easy make-ahead should be flavorful enough to please the former and light enough to suit the latter.

> 2 medium onions, thinly sliced
> 2 tablespoons oil
> 4 garlic cloves, minced
> Salt and pepper to taste
> 6 medium zucchini, scrubbed and thinly sliced
> 1/4 cup lemon juice
> 1/3 cup chopped fresh parsley

In a 10" skillet, sauté onions in oil until barely golden.
Add garlic, salt and pepper and mix well.
Add zucchini and cook until tender, covering pan for part of the time so that vegetable juices do not evaporate. Add lemon juice and stir gently.
Garnish with parsley. Serve chilled or, preferably, at room temperature. Serves 6-8.

Polenta With Leek and Mushroom Topping

The Israelites wandering hungry in the desert longed for the savory vegetables they had eaten in Egypt: "...the cucumbers...the leeks, the onions and the garlic." (Num. 11, v.5) Although leeks have been known for millennia, they were hard to find in U.S. markets for most of this century. Happily, that has changed in the last few years. Try them with mushrooms and, like our forebears, you will long to eat them often.

72

1 1/2 cups coarsely chopped mushrooms
(about 6 ounces)
1 1/2 cups chopped leeks, white and palest green parts
only (about 3/4 pound, untrimmed)
4 teaspoons olive oil; more if needed
Salt and pepper

Heat oil in heavy skillet. Add leeks and cook slowly until they begin to show a little brown around the edges. Use a slotted spoon to remove leeks from skillet.

Add more oil, if necessary.
Add mushrooms and cook slowly. When they give up their juices, continue cooking until liquid evaporates. Return leeks to skillet and mix with mushrooms. Season to taste with salt and pepper. Serve on hot polenta or lightly toasted Italian bread. Serves 6-8.

Polenta
4 cups water, divided
1/2 teaspoon salt
1 1/4 cups cornmeal

Put 2 1/2 cups water in a heavy 3 or 4 quart pot. Bring to boil. Mix cornmeal with 1 1/2 cups cold water. (A bowl with a spout is ideal for this.) Pour cornmeal and water into the boiling water. Reduce the heat at once or you are likely to be scalded by volcanic eruptions of cornmeal. Simmer, stirring constantly, over low heat, about 35 minutes or until the mixture pulls away from the sides of the pan. Spread the polenta in an oiled (or non-stick) 10" pie pan.

When cool, cut the polenta in wedges, diamonds or squares. Preheat broiler. Arrange polenta on a lightly greased cookie sheet and broil about 3 minutes on each side or until it begins to brown. Top with leeks and mushrooms.
Serves 8.

Note: Polenta-making requires your constant presence, but not a lot of concentration. Set up your favorite CD or tape for diversion during the stirring time. (Prepared polenta, ready to grill, is now in many supermarkets. You may find it in the deli or cheese case.)

Variations: Other suggestions for topping: Serve with tomato sauce, chili, or ratatouille, or with a simple sauté of onions and red bell peppers. Also good topped with spinach with raisins and pine nuts. Nice for breakfast with stewed fruit, jam or syrup.

Lemon Lovers' Green Beans

Probably America's favorite cooked green vegetable, thus a safe bet for holiday guests. The citrus note raises it to festive status.

2 pounds fresh green beans, trimmed
Juice of 2 lemons, with a little bit of rind
2 tablespoons margarine
Salt and pepper to taste

Steam beans until just tender, about 8 minutes
In large skillet, melt margarine, sauté beans very quickly, adding lemon juice and rind as they cook. Add seasonings. Serve immediately. Serves 8.

Cranberry Nut Bars

1 cup quick-cooking oatmeal
3/4 cup brown sugar
1/2 cup sifted flour
1/2 cup coconut
1/3 cup margarine
1/2 cup chopped walnuts
1 pound can whole berry cranberry sauce
1 tablespoon lemon juice

Preheat oven to 350^0 F.
Mix oatmeal, sugar, flour and coconut. Cut in margarine until crumbly.
Place half this mixture into 9" square pan; pat down gently.

Mix nuts, cranberry sauce and lemon juice. Spread over mixture in pan. Cover with remaining crumb mixture. Bake about 35 minutes. Cut into 16 bars when cool.

SIMCHAT TORAH

Tishrei

Menu 1

Noodle and Mushroom Casserole
Lentil Hot Pot
Israeli Salad
Chocolate Pecan Cookies

Menu 2

Gingered Lentil Soup, or
Elegant Lentil Soup
Bruschetta with Avocado and
                        Tomato
Spinach with Pine Nuts and
                        Raisins
Barley Salad
Baked Apples

Recipes for Simchat Torah At A Glance:
Appetizers: *Curried Lentil Pâté, Black Bean and Red Pepper Salsa*
Soups: *Elegant Lentil Soup, Gingered Lentil Soup*
Entrées: *Lentil Pie with Mashed Potato Crust, Bruschetta with Avocado and Tomato, Zucchini With Love and Mint, Lentil Loaf, Noodle Mushroom Casserole*
Sauce: *Lentil Spaghetti Sauce*
Salads: *Spinach-Apricot salad, Spinach with Raisins and Pine Nuts, Israeli Salad*
Desserts: *Chocolate Pecan Cookies, Banana Cookies, Baked Apples*

Simchat Torah celebrates the giving of the Torah to the Jewish people. The sign of God's covenant with us is the rainbow, binding Jewish history to nature. The holiday gained importance during the Middle Ages and is now celebrated with singing, dancing and much joy. It is a good time to remember that the covenant is established between God and "...every living creature."

God said to Noah and to his sons, "I have established My covenant with you and your offspring to come, and with every living creature that is with you-- birds, cattle, and every wild beast as well--all that have come out of the ark, every living creature on earth. I will maintain My covenant with you....This is the sign that I set for the covenant between Me and you, and every living creature with you for all ages to come. I have set My bow in the clouds and it shall serve as a sign of the covenant between Me and the earth." (Gen. 9:9-16)

Lentils have a long pedigree stemming from the Bible and Mediterranean history, and human beings have been eating lentils for about 8,000 years. Scholars believe that they were first cultivated in Northeastern Iraq. This valuable source of protein played its part in the Bible. Abraham and Sarah most likely ate lentil dishes. The "mess of pottage," which Jacob offered to Esau in exchange for his birthright was undoubtedly lentils.

Curried Lentil Pâté

  1/2 package of uncooked lentils, cooked according to
        directions on package, or in appendix on beans
  2 tablespoons oil
  1 medium onion, chopped
  2 cloves garlic, minced
  2 teaspoons curry powder
  1/4 teaspoon turmeric
  1/2 teaspoon cumin seeds
  1/2 teaspoon salt
  1 cup lentils
  2 cups water

Heat oil in large saucepan. Sauté onions until translucent. Add remaining spices, mix together well, sauté 5 more minutes. Add lentils and water, bring to a boil, cover, reduce heat to low, and simmer for about 1 hour. Watch level of water. There should be just enough so that all the water is absorbed, but if it becomes too dry before lentils are cooked, add a bit more. Purée in blender.

Serve with a plain cracker or bread, to let the intense flavor of the paté come through.

Black Bean and Red Pepper Salsa

Served as an appetizer, this will wake up the taste buds. As a side dish or as part of a buffet it will perk up both plate and palate.

> 1 1/2 pounds red bell peppers, about 4 medium,
>   stemmed, seeded, deribbed, finely diced
> 1 cup finely chopped red onions
> 1 tablespoon minced garlic
> 2 tablespoons olive oil
> 1/3 cup fruity white wine
> 1/2 teaspoon dried oregano
> 15 ounce can black beans, drained and rinsed
> 1 teaspoon Tabasco (or to taste)
> 1 tablespoon fresh lemon or lime juice
> 3 tablespoons chopped fresh cilantro sprigs
> Salt and freshly ground pepper

Garnish: Chopped fresh avocado and cilantro sprigs, optional

Heat olive oil in a 10" skillet over moderate heat. Add peppers and onions and sauté until vegetables start to soften, about 3-4 minutes. Add garlic and sauté one minute.

Add wine and oregano and cook 3-4 more minutes, until vegetables are tender, but still have a little bite.

Remove from heat, cool, stir in beans, Tabasco, lime juice and cilantro.
Add salt and pepper to taste. Add garnishes, if desired. Serve as plated salad, or as a dip with pita toasts. Serves 8.

Elegant Lentil Soup

Easy to make and very healthy: low in fat, high in fiber and flavor.

1 pound package of lentils cooked according to soup directions on package, but substitute 1/2 cup sherry for 1/2 cup water.

Gingered Lentil Soup

The unexpected crunch and zing of ginger in this recipe adds an eye-opening contemporary twist to this ancient soup.

2 tablespoons olive oil
1 large onion, chopped (1-1/2-2 cups)
3-6 cloves garlic, chopped
3-4 tablespoons fresh ginger root,
                 peeled, diced or grated
3-4 carrots, peeled and diced
3 1/2 cups water, divided
1 pound brown lentils, rinsed and drained
6 cups vegetable stock
Salt and freshly ground pepper to taste
Splashes of balsamic vinegar, to taste

In 6 to 8 quart or larger stock pot, warm oil over medium heat. Sauté onion, garlic and ginger until transparent. Add 2/3 cup of the water along with the carrots, simmer a minute or two. Add lentils, stock, and remaining water, and partially cover the pot. Simmer about 30-40 minutes, stirring often, until lentils have melted and soup is thick. Remove from heat and rest briefly. Add seasonings and vinegar to taste. Serves 8. Freezes well.

Lentil Pie With Mashed Potato Crust

2 cups brown lentils, to yield 4 cups cooked
1 tablespoon oil
2 medium onions, chopped
2 tablespoons chopped fresh parsley
3 ribs celery, chopped
5 cloves, garlic, mashed
1 large carrot, grated
1 teaspoon cumin
1 teaspoon curry
1/4 teaspoon turmeric
Salt and freshly ground pepper, to taste
3 large tomatoes, diced
1 cup water
1 tablespoon tomato paste

Topping:
3 large potatoes, peeled, and cut in quarters
A few tablespoonfuls of potato cooking water
or soy milk
1 tablespoon oil or margarine (optional)
Salt and freshly ground pepper to taste
Paprika

Cook lentils according to directions in Appendix, About Beans

Meanwhile, make the topping. Put potatoes in medium pot with cold water to cover. Bring to boil, reduce to simmer and cook until tender, 20-40 minutes. Test for doneness. Drain, reserving a little cooking water. Mash or put through ricer. Add a little cooking water or soy milk, and optional margarine to make smooth, cohesive, mashed potatoes. Season to taste.

In medium skillet, warm oil and sauté onions, garlic, celery, carrot, parsley, cumin, curry, turmeric, salt and pepper for 5 minutes. Add tomatoes. Mix water with tomato paste and add to skillet. Mix well, simmer 15 minutes.

Preheat oven to 350^0 F.
In a large bowl, mix cooked vegetables with lentils and spoon into greased
 9" x 12" baking dish. Top with mashed potatoes, smoothing with a spatula. Sprinkle with paprika. Bake 40 minutes until crust is firm and lightly brown. Serves 6-8.

Bruschetta With Avocado and Tomato

2 large avocados, peeled, in large dice
4 tomatoes, diced
1-2 garlic cloves, mashed or put through press
1-2 tablespoons lemon juice
Salt, optional
8 slices sourdough bread

Preheat broiler.
In medium bowl, mix first five ingredients. Spoon mixture over bread. Place on baking sheet and broil until edges of bread begin to brown. Serves 8.

Zucchini With Love and Mint

Mint has a long association with love. In Greek mythology, a nymph dallying with Pluto was turned into mint by his jealous wife, Persephone. It takes love of quite a different kind to tend the skillet with the care necessary to make this dish. Like the legend, it is memorable and comes to us from a family that has treasured it for generations. Rosa's friend, Barbara Beckett Giordano, received this recipe from her Italian mother-in-law, who learned to make it in her home village near Milan.

> 6 unbruised zucchini (each about 8" long)
> 6-8 tablespoons olive oil
> 2/3 cup fresh mint leaves, minced
> 2 tablespoons plus 2 teaspoons finely chopped garlic
> 1/3 cup red wine vinegar and 1 cup water
> mixed in a 2 cup measure
> Salt

Trim zucchini ends and slice into rounds about 1/8" thick. Cover the bottom of a large skillet with the olive oil and heat until oil begins to smoke. Lay as many zucchini rounds as will fit edge to edge. Turn each round as it blisters and becomes tinged with brown. When the second side of each one is toasted, remove to a bowl for marinating. Put more zucchini rounds into the pan. While the second batch is frying, dress those in the bowl with a sprinkle of salt, a generous spread of mint leaves, some of the chopped garlic and a good splash of the watered vinegar. Continue frying and dressing until all ingredients are used. Mix the marinating zucchini with a gentle tossing motion. Serve right away at room temperature, or marinate for up to two days in refrigerator. Return to room temperature to serve. The volume of zucchini will reduce considerably, but it will be enough for 8 moderate portions.

Note: Don't even think about making this with dried mint!

Lentil Loaf

There are many versions of lentil loaf, but we like this one offered by The Vegetarian Resource Group. We recommend it for dinner, and it keeps well for the next day. Serve leftover cool or at room temperature. Makes excellent sandwiches with mustard or ketchup.

1 cup uncooked lentils, cooked according
   to directions on package, or in appendix on beans
2 cups tomato sauce
1/2 cup onions, chopped
1/2 cup celery chopped
3/4 cup rolled oats
1/2 teaspoon garlic powder
1/4 teaspoon Italian seasoning
1/4 teaspoon celery seed
Pepper and salt to taste
1/2 cup walnuts, chopped (optional)
2-3 drops of hot Chinese oil, optional

Preheat oven to 350^0 F.
Mix all ingredients together in a large bowl. Press into lightly oiled, 5 1/2" x 11" loaf pan. Bake 45 minutes. Cool slightly, 5-8 minutes. Slice. Serves 8. Delicious cold the next day. Can be served in sandwiches.

Tip: Crumble and reheat leftover loaf with sautéed mushrooms and serve over rice.

Lentil Spaghetti Sauce
Makes pasta a healthy gourmet dish.

1/2 cup uncooked lentils, cooked according to directions on package,
   or in appendix on beans
1/2 pound sliced mushrooms
2 coarsely diced medium tomatoes
1/2 teaspoon thyme
1/2 teaspoon chili powder
Salt and pepper to taste
4 ounces tomato sauce, optional

Sauté mushrooms and tomatoes. Add herbs and seasoning. Add tomato sauce, if desired. Mix with cooked lentils. Spoon over spaghetti.

Noodle and Mushroom Casserole

      4 medium onions, chopped
      4 tablespoons oil
      1 1/2 pounds mushrooms, trimmed and sliced
      Salt and pepper to taste
      1 package (12 or 16 ounces) fettucine
      1 cup cornflake crumbs

Preheat oven to 350^0 F.
Heat oil in a large skillet. Add onions and sauté until tender and translucent. Add mushrooms and cook until tender.

Break fettucine into 2" or 3" lengths. Cook in boiling water until tender. Drain. Add to skillet, tossing gently. Add about half the cornflake crumbs and toss again.

Spoon mixture into an oiled 9" x 13" baking dish. top with remaining crumbs. Bake, covered for 30-45 minutes. Serves 12.

Note: Plain, white mushrooms are fine. Brown Crimini mushrooms give the dish a dark, rich look.

Spinach-Apricot Salad

"I say it's spinach....and it's heavenly...."
Bruce Silverlieb, The Party Specialist, demonstrated this for a sisterhood cooking meeting as part of a brunch menu. It drew unanimous raves. It's a salad worthy of the rejoicing of this holiday.

      1 6 ounce package dried apricots, sliced
      1 1 pound package fresh spinach
      3 tablespoons vinegar (preferably raspberry)
      3 tablespoons apricot preserves
      1/2 cup vegetable oil
      3/4 cup toasted macadamia nuts

In a small bowl, plump the apricots in the boiling water. Let them stand about 30 minutes or until softened. Drain well.

Remove stems from spinach; wash leaves thoroughly and pat dry. Tear into bite-size pieces and place in serving bowl.

In blender, process vinegar and preserves until smooth. With blender on high, gradually add oil in a slow, steady stream.

Add half the apricots and nuts and all the dressing to the spinach. Toss gently. Sprinkle with remaining apricots and nuts. Serve immediately. Serves 8.

Spinach with Raisins and Pine Nuts

    4 tablespoons olive oil
    1/3 cup pine nuts
    2 medium onions finely chopped
    2 cloves garlic, minced
    4 pounds fresh spinach, washed and stemmed
    1/2 cup raisins, plumped in boiling water, drained
    Salt and freshly ground black pepper

Heat olive oil in 10" skillet. Add pine nuts and sauté, stirring until golden. Remove nuts with slotted spoon and set aside.
Add onions to skillet and sauté until tender and golden. Add garlic and sauté one minute. Remove skillet from heat and set aside.

In a large covered pot, cook the spinach for 5 or 6 minutes in the water remaining on the leaves after washing. Stir the pot from top to bottom occasionally. Drain in a colander; use the back of a spoon to press out all the liquid, or squeeze it out by hand. Chop spinach coarsely and add to skillet. Add raisins and nuts, reserving a few nuts for garnish. Season to taste with salt and pepper. Reheat. Remove to serving dish. Sprinkle remaining nuts on top. Serves 8-10. Leftovers are good at room temperature.

Note: Spinach loses volume drastically in cooking. One pound reduces to about 1 cup or 2 servings.

Israeli Salad

This salad is the glory of the kibbutz table, the favorite of all Israelis, and has played a major role in creating the Sabra image. In fact, in Israel, salad is macho. On the kibbutz, the diet was carbohydrate-and-plant-based as had been the historical food of the human race. Jews in Israel underwent a major dietary change in their migration from eastern Europe to Israel, and the results are evident in their physical appearance.

3 large tomatoes or 5 medium plum tomatoes
2 large regular cucumbers, or 3 pickling cucumbers, or
1 English cucumber
1 green pepper, seeded, deribbed and diced
1/2 cup chopped mild onion,
or 1/3 cup chopped scallions
1 large carrot , grated (optional)
A few radishes, finely sliced (optional)

Cut the tomatoes in eighths, or the plum tomatoes in quarters or sixths. Over a large bowl, hold a tomato wedge and cut it into large dice, allowing the juices to drip into the bowl.

Peel the cucumbers, unless using the English cucumber. Cut into strips and then into medium dice. Add to tomatoes along with onion, green pepper, and optional vegetables.

Dressing:
1 tablespoon vegetable oil
2 tablespoons lemon juice or wine vinegar
1/4 cup chopped parsley (optional)
2 tablespoons snipped dill (optional)
Salt and pepper to taste

Add oil to salad and toss gently. Add remaining ingredients and toss again. Chill until serving time. Serves 4-6.

Chocolate Pecan Cookies

The most luscious of the nut cookies.

>1 cup unbleached all-purpose flour
>2 tablespoons potato starch
>1/4 teaspoon salt
>2 1/3 cups pecan halves
>9 ounces semi-sweet or bittersweet chocolate
>1 cup unsalted margarine, cut into 16 equal parts
>1 teaspoon vanilla extract
>1 1/4 cups confectioners sugar

Place flour, potato starch, salt, and half of the pecans in a food processor fitted with the metal blade and process until the pecans are finely chopped. Remove from processor and set aside.

Process the chocolate for about one minute, until it is finely chopped.

In a small saucepan, melt half the margarine. Start the processor, and pour the melted margarine through the feed tube.

Add vanilla, sugar, and remaining margarine. Process for 5 seconds. Scrape down the bowl. Add reserved pecan-flour mixture and pulse 10-12 times until well mixed, scraping down the bowl as necessary.

Refrigerate dough for 1 hour or longer . (Dough can be prepared the day before.)

Preheat oven to 300^0 F. Position oven racks in center of oven.

Use a heaping teaspoon of dough for each cookie. Roll into balls and place about 2" apart on ungreased cookie sheets. Top each cookie with a pecan half. Bake until firm, about 15-20 minutes.

Let cookies cool briefly on the sheets. With broad metal spatula, remove to cooling rack. If the first cookie crumbles, wait a minute or two longer before trying again. Makes about 10 dozen cookies.

Note: Chocolate bits can be used in place of the chocolate bar, but you will still have to grind them.

Baked Apples

1 apple per person (Granny Smith or Cortland)

For each apple: 2-3 teaspoons white or brown sugar
1 teaspoon chopped walnuts
2 teaspoons dried cranberries or dark raisins
1/2 teaspoon margarine
1 tablespoon water or apple juice

Peel a 1 1/2" strip from the top of each apple. Mix remaining ingredients, except liquid, and fill apple cavity.

Preheat oven to 350^0 F.
Arrange apples in baking pan just large enough to hold them without crowding. Pour water or juice around them. Bake for 45 minutes, or until just tender, basting occasionally.

Banana Cookies

These dense, chewy cookies are easy to stir up. Children can help shape and finish them. Unlike most of the cookies in this book, they contain no nuts or peanuts and are excellent for allergic cookie lovers. However, they do not keep well. The yield is small, so that should not be a problem.

1 1/4 cups flour
1/2 teaspoon baking powder
1/4 teaspoon salt
1/2 cup sugar
Dash of cinnamon
2 tablespoons oil
1 mashed banana, about 1/3 cup
2 or 3 teaspoons water
1 teaspoon grated lemon rind
1 tablespoon cinnamon plus 1/2 teaspoon sugar
1/3 cup apricot jam, divided

Stir flour, baking powder, salt, sugar and cinnamon in medium bowl. Add banana and oil to middle of bowl and stir until well blended, adding water as needed to make a pliable dough.

Preheat oven to 375^0 F.

Spread a sheet of waxed paper on a work surface. Make 1" balls of the cookie dough, placing them on the waxed paper. Flatten them slightly with fingers or the oiled bottom of a glass. Sprinkle liberally with cinnamon. Remove cookies to an oiled baking sheet.

Use the back of a 1/4 teaspoon measure to make a dimple in the middle of each cookie. Fill the hollows with a little of the jam. Bake 10 minutes. Remove from oven and reduce heat to 350^0 F. Stir jam, adding a few drops of water if necessary to thin it. With a pastry brush, apply a thin coat of jam to the cookies. Return to oven and bake 5 minutes more. Cool on racks. Makes about 18 cookies.

CHANUKAH

Kislev

Menu 1
Potato Latkes
 Gourmet Applesauce for Latkes
Best or Gourmet Burgers on Rolls
    with Choice of Condiments
Sweet and Sour Red Cabbage
Banana Fudge Rolls

Menu 2
Black Bean soup
Pasta With Peanut-Sesame Sauce
Marinated Cucumber Salad
Pears in Red Wine

Recipes for Chanukah At a Glance:
Appetizers: Potato Latkes With Gourmet Applesauce, Knishes
Soups: Black Bean Soup, Classic Borscht
Entrées: Best Burgers, Gourmet Burgers with Mushrooms, Bean and Corn
Tamale Pie, Spicy Peanut Pasta, Onion Tart
Side Dishes: Curried Potatoes and Apples, Sweet and Sour Red Cabbage
Salad: Marinated Cucumbers
Desserts: Banana Fudge Roll, Applesauce Muffins, Pears In Red Wine

It is a mitzvah to light candles on Chanukah. In some families, every member has a personal chanukiah. It can be fun for children and other creative individuals to make their own chanukiot. The eight holders for candles or oil must be on one level, the ninth holder, the shamash, on another level. Heatproof material may be used. In poor communities, egg shell halves have been used to hold the oil.

A most unusual chanukiah was a temporary makeshift one described by Edda Servi Machlin in *The Classic Cuisine of the Italian Jews.* In 1944, when the American army arrived in Tuscany, Jews came out of their hiding places. On the last night of Chanukah, a Jewish soldier invited the Servi family to his camp where the rabbi had made a chanukiah from eight helmets on the ground, each topped with a candle. Two more helmets stacked in the middle held the shamash---new light, new hope in a dark time.

Like Pesach and Purim, Chanukah acquires new meaning in different eras. The following passage is from *A Treasure Hunt in Judaism,* a children's book by Rabbi Harold P. Smith, published during World War II.

"The year 5702 or 1942, finds the name of Antiochus Epiphanes practically forgotten, merely annoying religious school pupils who try to pronounce or spell it. The Chanukah candles, however, burn just as brightly as they did 2100 years ago, and they will burn just as brightly 2100 years from now when such names as Adolf Hitler, together with that of Antiochus Epiphanes, will be filed among the nightmares of history."

Chanukah commemorates the defeat of the mighty Syrian tyrant Antiochus 1V by the small band of Maccabees in the year 165 B.C.E. The victors found the temple desecrated, the Eternal Light extinguished, and only one day's supply of holy oil remaining. They cleansed and rededicated the temple. "Chanukah" means "dedication." They relit the lamp and sent for more oil. Although there was only enough oil for one day, tradition tells us that the lamp miraculously kept burning until more oil arrived eight days later.

In its earliest years, Chanukah contained elements of the Sukkot celebration. After restoring the temple, the Maccabees, who had been unable to observe Sukkot in their mountain hideouts, brought the lulav there and offered psalms of thanksgiving and praise. This link with our harvest festival gives meaning to the vegetable and grain dishes in our Chanukah meals.

Judah Maccabee never ate a latke, he never even saw a potato. Potatoes did not reach Europe until the Conquistadors brought them from Peru and Ecuador in the sixteenth century, and they did not come into widespread use in Europe or the Middle East until two hundred years later. By then, the custom of eating foods cooked with oil on Chanukah was long established.

As for the potato, once on the scene, the latke became the undisputed star of the Ashkenazic Chanukah menu. Among Sephardim, the best-known dishes are fried pastries such as Iranian *zelebis* and Greek or Turkish *bimuelos*. Israelis make jelly-filled doughnuts called *soufganiot*. Italian Jews eat a dish made of rice with garlic, raisins, and olive oil. Syrian Jews make a rich, luscious bulgur pilaf called *bazerghan*. Jews of the Baghdadi-Indian community make a *halwa* from semolina (quite unlike the familiar sesame halva).

Chanukah is an excellent time to remember the merits and traditions of the olive tree, and olive dishes should be as common during Chanukah as latkes, for it is the miracle of olive oil that we celebrate. In his book, *In Search of Plenty, A History of Jewish Food,* Oded Schwartz, writes, "The association [of Chanukah] with oil may also stem from the fact that Chanukah coincides with the end of the olive harvest when olive oil is plentiful." (p. 76-77)

Chanukah is a holiday for children and parties, full of lights and small presents. When Roberta's children were small, they made a "Chanukah mobile," of Maccabee soldiers and oil lamps which they cut from colored oak tag paper. They strung it up with chocolate Chanukah *gelt* which they ate at the end of the holiday. For each of the eight nights, after candle lighting, they searched for a small gift that was hidden away. The gift was modest. It was the search that made the gift memorable. The whole family played "hot and cold" as the children ran through the house in their pajamas after the lighting of the candles.

Potato Latkes

2 cups stale bread, torn in medium size pieces
2 raw baking potatoes
1 to 2 teaspoons salt
1/2 small onion, grated
Pepper to taste
Oil for cooking

Soak bread in cold water for a few minutes, then squeeze out the water. Grate potatoes by hand or in food processor. If using processor, first use the grating disk, then empty work bowl and reprocess briefly, using the steel cutting blade.

Combine potatoes, bread, onion and seasonings in medium bowl.
Heat thin layer of oil in skillet. Drop batter by spoonfuls, using back of spoon to shape the latkes neatly. Fry until crisp and brown on both sides. Makes 6-8. Recipe can easily be doubled.

Variations: Grate a zucchini and/or two scallions into the grated potatoes to make a lighter, spicier latke.

Gourmet Applesauce for Latkes

With a sprinkling of nutmeg on top, this is a happy childhood memory. And of course it is the essential complement to latkes.

> 6 apples (Cortlands, Granny Smiths, or Macs)
> Water
> 1/4 cup sugar, or less
> Lemon juice to taste (optional)

Quarter the apples and place in pot with water almost to cover. Bring to a boil over medium high heat, reduce to simmer, cook until tender, about 10 minutes. Put through a food mill. Add sugar and lemon juice to taste, if needed. Simmer about 3 minutes or until slightly thickened. Makes about 4 cups.

Variations: 1) Pare and core the apples, and you will not need to put them through the food mill. Just mash them with a potato masher until smooth.
2) Add a 2" piece of cinnamon stick to the apples during cooking. Remove before mashing or milling. Use brown sugar, or a mixture of brown and white sugar.

Knishes

These knishes resemble tiny turnovers. They are a terrific treat for parties and a top-notch accompaniment to soups anytime. The recipe looks long because we offer three fillings, but it's really quite simple and you can make the components a day or two ahead--or make the complete recipe and freeze. Great to have on hand for unexpected guests.

Potato Dough Knishes

3 large baking potatoes, peeled and quartered
(enough for dough and filling)
1 tablespoon or more potato cooking water,
stock or soy milk

Other Dough Ingredients:

3 tablespoons margarine
3 tablespoons vegetable shortening
1 cup flour
1/2 teaspoon salt
Dash pepper

In medium saucepan, bring to boil potatoes and water to cover. Reduce heat, cover, and simmer until potatoes are tender, about 15 minutes. Drain well, return to pan, and shake gently over low heat to dry.

Mash potatoes in the pan with a fork or masher, adding seasonings and enough liquid to hold them together. Measure one cup of mashed potatoes for dough and reserve remainder for filling.

To make the dough: In a small mixing bowl cut shortening and margarine into flour with pastry blender or two knives. When well combined, add measured cup of mashed potatoes and mix well. Form the dough into a ball, wrap in plastic wrap, and chill at least 20 minutes. May be kept overnight. Makes enough pastry for about 2 dozen small knishes.

Potato-Onion Filling:
1 1/2-2 cups mashed potatoes
1-1 1/2 cups chopped onions
1 tablespoon oil
Salt and freshly ground black pepper

Heat oil in medium saucepan or skillet. Sauté onions until tender and lightly browned. Mix onions with mashed potatoes. Season to taste with salt and pepper.

Mushroom Filling:

2 cups mushrooms, finely chopped
1 onion, finely chopped
2 tablespoons oil, divided
Salt and freshly ground black pepper

Heat 1 tablespoon oil in medium skillet. Add onion and sauté until tender and lightly browned. Remove onions with slotted spoon, set aside, and add remaining oil to pan. Add mushrooms and sauté, stirring, until tender. Combine mushrooms and onions and season to taste with salt and pepper.

Kasha and Onion Filling:

1/2 cup buckwheat groats (kasha)
2 tablespoons oil, divided
1 cup boiling water
1 onion, finely chopped
Salt and freshly ground black pepper

Heat 1 tablespoon oil in medium non-stick skillet. Toast kasha in the oil, stirring constantly for about 2 minutes. Add boiling water, cover and cook about 7 minutes. Remove from heat. Some water will remain in bottom of the pot. Let sit a few minutes until all water is absorbed. Stir to separate grains. Let sit, uncovered at room temperature 15-20 minutes, stirring a few times to keep grains separate.

Heat remaining oil in a small skillet. Add onions and sauté until tender and golden. Mix with kasha. Season to taste with salt and pepper.

To Assemble the Knishes:

Preheat oven to 400^0 F.
Lightly flour rolling pin and work surface. Roll out dough, making a thin sheet, about 1/8" thick. Use a cookie cutter to make 3" rounds. Place a heaping teaspoon of filling on each round. Moisten half of the outer edge of *(Continued)*

each round with a pastry brush or finger dipped in a little water. Fold rounds over in half-moon shapes and seal, pressing edges together with back of fork. Prick tops with fork. Bake on greased cookie sheet for 20 minutes or until golden brown. Watch carefully for the last few minutes to make sure they don't burn. Makes about 24 small knishes.

Black Bean Soup

 We like the way small amounts of several assertive flavors blend to produce the distinctive taste of this soup without overwhelming the beans. The list of ingredients is given in two sections, as there are two separate mixtures to be combined at the end. The effort is worthwhile.

1 pound black beans
2 tablespoons olive oil
1 ripe medium tomato
1 bay leaf
1/2 medium onion
1/2 medium green pepper, seeded
1 garlic clove, crushed, not peeled
8 cups water

4 tablespoons olive oil
1/2 medium onion, chopped
1/2 green pepper, seeded, deribbed and chopped
1 garlic clove, minced
1 teaspoon crushed oregano
1/2 teaspoon cumin
2 tablespoons wine vinegar
2 tablespoons salt or to taste
1/2 teaspoon hot sauce or chili oil
2 tablespoons dry sherry, optional
1 cup chopped raw mild onion, optional
2 cups cooked white rice (1 cup raw)

Pick over the beans, discard foreign matter or shrivelled beans. Soak beans overnight in a deep bowl, in water 2 inches above the beans.

Drain and rinse beans, place them in a 3 or 4 quart pot. Add 8 cups water, the olive oil, tomato, bay leaf, onion half, green pepper half, and crushed garlic. Bring to boil, reduce heat to simmer and cover. Cook about 1 hour or until beans are tender. Stir occasionally. (*Continued*)

When beans are tender, remove the bay leaf, the onion and pepper halves, and tomato with a slotted spoon, pressing their juices into the pan as you do so. If possible, mash the garlic clove into the soup. Remove 2 cups or more of the soup, purée it in a food processor or blender, and return to pot. (If a thicker soup is preferred, purée a larger amount.)

In a small skillet, heat 4 tablespoons olive oil, and sauté the chopped onion and pepper until onion is transparent and pepper is limp. Add the garlic, oregano, cumin, wine vinegar and salt. Stir briefly, cook 2 minutes longer and add to soup. Add the hot sauce, cover and simmer half an hour. Correct seasonings. add sherry, if desired. Serve over white rice. Garnish with raw onion, if desired. Serves 8.

Classic Borscht

A soup for all seasons.

3 large or 4 medium fresh beets, peeled, diced or
    coarsely grated
Juice of 1 lemon, approximately, divided in half
Salt
Pinch of sour salt (or up to 2 teaspoons, to taste)
1 onion, chopped
1 tablespoon to 1/3 cup sugar, or to taste
2 quarts water or vegetable broth
Optional garnishes: boiled potatoes, chopped scallions,
    minced fresh dill

In 3 quart saucepan, combine and bring to boil water or vegetable broth, beets, onion, juice of half a lemon, dash of salt and sour salt. Reduce heat and simmer covered until beets are tender, about 40 minutes.

Add juice of another half lemon. Taste and add lemon and sugar as needed, until the flavors are balanced. Cook another 10 minutes. Taste again. Adjust seasonings as needed.

Cool soup, put through processor or blender to obtain texture preferred. (Best if not puréed too fine.) Serve hot with potatoes, chopped scallions and dill. Yields approximately 1 1/2 quarts. Serves 6-8.

Best Burgers

A succulent contribution from The North American Vegetarian Society to burger cuisine. The mixture needs to cool for at least an hour before being shaped and baked, so plan accordingly. Batter can be made hours in advance.

> 4 1/2 cups of water
> 1/2 cup soy sauce
> 1/3 cup oil, or 1/2 cup chopped nuts
> 1/4 teaspoon Italian seasoning
> 1/4 cup flaked nutritional yeast
> 2-3 drops hot Chinese oil, optional
> 1 large onion, finely chopped with 2 garlic cloves
> 4 1/2 cups rolled oats

In 2 1/2 or 3 quart saucepan, bring all ingredients except oats to a boil. Reduce heat and add oats. Do not stir. Let it absorb liquid. Cook on very low heat 5 minutes. Cool batter at least one hour and turn once to make sure they are all moistened.

Preheat oven to 350^0 F.
Form into patties, place on oiled tray, bake 45 minutes, turning once. Makes about 16 medium size burgers.

Gourmet Burgers With Mushrooms

An elegant variation on Best Burgers, also from the North American Vegetarian Society.

> 1/2 pound fresh mushrooms, diced
> 1 large onion, diced
> 1/4 cup oil
> 1/2 teaspoon salt
> 4 1/2 cups water
> 1/3 cup soy sauce
> 1 teaspoon garlic powder
> 1/4 teaspoon oregano
> 1/2 teaspoon dried basil
> 1/2 teaspoon thyme
> 1/4 cup brewer's yeast (powder or flake)
> 5 cups old-fashioned rolled oats

Sauté first two ingredients in oil in a large saucepan. Add salt. In another large saucepan, bring to a boil the other ingredients, except the oats. Lower heat, add sautéed vegetables.

Add oats, one cup at a time. Allow each cupful to sink a little before stirring gently. Cook five minutes, until mixture starts to stick to bottom of the pot. Set aside to cool at least 15 minutes, or until mixture can be handled.

Preheat oven to 350^0 F.
Form patties and place on oiled cookie sheet. Bake for about 45 minutes. Turn once after 20 minutes. Makes 20-25 burgers.

Variations: Chopped dill or parsley added to seasonings.

Bean and Corn Tamale Pie

Advance Preparation Tip: Make the vegetable mixture, without the corn, a day or two ahead. Add corn just before baking.

> 1 large green pepper, chopped
> 1 onion, chopped
> 2 cloves garlic, minced
> 1 1/2 tablespoons vegetable oil
> 3/4 cup chopped pitted black olives
> 3 1/2 cups whole canned tomatoes,
>   with some of their juice
> 1 1/2 tablespoons chili powder, or to taste
> 1/4 teaspoon red pepper sauce, optional
> 1 teaspoon salt
> 1/8 teaspoon freshly ground black pepper
> 2 1/2 cups cooked kidney or pinto beans
> 2 1/2 cups whole kernel corn
> 1 1/2 cups cornmeal
> 4 1/2 cups water, divided
> 3/4 teaspoon salt
> 1/2 cup breadcrumbs, optional

In 10" or 12" skillet, heat the oil and sauté the green pepper and onion until onion is translucent and green pepper is limp, stirring occasionally. Add garlic and sauté one minute. Add tomatoes, breaking them up with a wooden spoon.

(Continued)

Add the beans, and mash them coarsely with a potato masher. Add olives, chili powder, pepper sauce, salt and pepper. Add enough juice from tomatoes to create a stew-like mixture that is moist, but not too soupy.

Reduce heat and simmer, covered, 15 minutes.

Meanwhile, boil 2 1/4 cups water in a 2 quart saucepan.

Mix cornmeal with 1 1/2 cups cold water and 3/4 teaspoon salt. Add to boiling water, stirring constantly. Cook, stirring frequently over medium heat until thickened, about 15 to 20 minutes.

Preheat oven to 350^0 F.
Oil a 13" x 9" x 2" baking dish and spread the cooked cornmeal over its bottom and sides. Add the corn kernels to the vegetable mixture, stir well, and spoon into the crust. Sprinkle with bread crumbs, if desired. Bake 30 minutes. Serves 8-10.

Spicy Peanut Pasta

During Chanukah, we often have much company, and often the company is young and hungry and needs a zippy, filling dish. This dish is always a big hit at home or away. It's a favorite for your own party, or to take as a potluck dish. It travels well and when it arrives everyone loves it and asks for the recipe. For larger groups, it can be multiplied easily.

> 3/4-1 cup chunky peanut butter
> 8 tablespoons soy sauce or tamari
> 6 tablespoons dark sesame oil
> 4 tablespoons red wine vinegar
> 4 teaspoons sugar
> 2-4 teaspoons chili paste with garlic
> 6-8 tablespoons hot pasta cooking water
> 1 pound thin spaghetti
> 1/2 pound scallions, trimmed
> 1/4 cup chopped roasted peanuts

In a large bowl, combine peanut butter, soy or tamari, sesame oil, red wine vinegar, sugar, and chili paste with garlic.Mince half the scallions. You should have about one-half cup. Set aside. Mince the rest of the scallions, keeping white and green parts separate.

Cook spaghetti al dente, following package instructions. When done, ladle out 3/4 cup of cooking water and reserve. Drain pasta, rinse briefly under cold water, drain again.

Add 6-8 tablespoons of reserved cooking water to mixture in bowl, stirring to mix thoroughly. Add the pasta and the mixed-color scallions to the sauce. Toss gently until the strands are uniformly coated with sauce. If sauce is too thick, add a little more cooking water.

Remove to a large serving bowl. Make an attractive bull's eye pattern on top of the pasta with the white and green parts of the scallions and the chopped peanuts. Serve at room temperature. Serves 6-8.

Tip: Avoid salty peanut butter.

Onion Tart

This pie is so colorful, it can serve as a centerpiece for a Chanukah table lit with candles.

Crust for Pizza Shell:
2 3/4 cups bread flour
1 teaspoon salt
1 teaspoon active dried yeast
1 teaspoon sugar
1 cup warm water
1 tablespoon olive oil

Stir flour and salt into a medium bowl.
In another small bowl combine yeast, sugar and 1/4 cup water; let stand until frothy. Add this yeast liquid, remaining water and the oil to flour mixture. Mix to a soft dough. Knead on a floured surface 10 minutes until smooth. Place in a greased bowl, and cover with a plastic wrap. Let rise in a warm place 45 minutes or until doubled in size.

Filling:
6 cups sliced onions
1 clove garlic chopped (optional)
1/4 cup olive oil
Salt and ground pepper
1/2 green bell pepper, cut in strips
1/2 red or yellow bell pepper, cut in strips
16 pitted black or green Mediterranean olives

Preheat oven to 500^0 F

Make a 10" pizza shell and partially bake at 500^0 F for five minutes. Reduce oven to 425^0 F. In a large, heavy saucepan, cook the onions and garlic in oil very slowly for 30-35 minutes or until completely tender and golden brown and sweet. Season with salt and pepper. Cool. You should end up with approximately 3 cups of onions. Scatter onions over the tart shell. Arrange pepper strips, fanning them out from the center. Place olives as you like. Bake for 15-20 minutes, or until filling is hot and pastry is browned. Cut into wedges and serve hot. Serves 8-10.

Curried Potatoes and Apples

A different way to serve potatoes during Chanukah, with less frying.

4 medium size potatoes in large dice
3 medium size Macintosh apples, peeled and sliced
1 teaspoon curry powder
1 pinch of ginger
1-3 tablespoons margarine or oil
(or spray for bottom of skillet)

Cook potatoes in boiling water until just tender. Meantime, sauté apples in oiled skillet until just soft.

Drain potatoes (if desired, reserve liquid for stock). Add to apples in skillet. Add curry powder and ginger. Mix gently, but well so that spices coat potatoes and apples. Serves 6.

Variation: Add 1/2 cup raisins or 1/2 cup slivered almonds--or both. If you add more ingredients, you may have to increase spices.

Sweet and Sour Red Cabbage

4 pounds red cabbage
1/3 cup vegetable oil
1 apple, preferably Granny Smith, peeled and diced
1/3 cup vinegar
1/2 cup currant jelly mixed with 1/2 cup water
1 1/2 teaspoons salt
1/4 cup sugar

100

Discard any tough outer leaves, and shred cabbage fine. Warm the oil in a large, heavy pot. Add the cabbage and apple. Cover and cook 5 minutes, shaking the pan frequently. Add the vinegar, currant jelly mixed with water, salt and sugar. Stir to combine thoroughly. Cook, covered, over low heat for 2 hours, stirring frequently and adding a little water if necessary. Taste and adjust the balance of sweet and sour to your liking. Serves 8-12.

Marinated Cucumber Salad

Plan ahead for this recipe, because it takes 3-7 days to marinate.

12 cucumbers, peeled, thinly sliced
1 large onion, thinly sliced
1 green pepper, seeded, deribbed, thinly sliced
2 cups vinegar
1 cup sugar
1 tablespoon salt
1 1/2 teaspoons pepper
1 garlic clove, or more to taste, peeled and quartered

Spear the garlic pieces on toothpicks. Combine all ingredients in large bowl and marinate, covered in refrigerator for 3-7 days. Remove garlic before serving. Serves at least 12.

Banana Fudge Roll

3/4 cup light unsweetened carob powder
2 teaspoons unsweetened apple or orange juice
2 cups crunchy peanut butter
1/2 cup honey
1 ripe banana, mashed
1 cup coarsely ground unsweetened coconut
Handfuls of additional coconut and granola, optional

Combine carob powder and juice in large bowl. Mix in peanut butter and honey, mash in banana. Stir in coconut and distribute evenly. Refrigerate for 1/2 hour.

On a wax paper-lined cookie sheet, shape dough into an 18" log. *(Continued)*

Sprinkle granola or coconut on the log. Roll log to cover evenly.
Re-wrap in the waxed paper used for shaping.

Chill for several hours, slice with a sharp, wet knife.
Makes about 48 pieces (3 slices per inch). Serve immediately.

Applesauce Muffins

You can prepare the dry and wet ingredients separately the evening before
baking these. Cover and refrigerate the liquid mixture. Sift the dry ingredients
in the mixing bowl, cover, and keep at room temperature. A good dish for
breakfast, lunch, or Chanukah party.

> 1 cup applesauce
> 1/2 cup molasses
> 1/4 cup oil
> 1 1/2 cups flour
> 3/4 teaspoon cinnamon
> 1/2 teaspoon baking soda
> 1/2 teaspoon salt
> Pinch of salt
> 1/2 teaspoon baking powder
> 1/2 cup raisins
> 1/2 cup chopped walnuts or pecans

Preheat oven to 375^0 F. Grease 12 2" muffin tin cups. Sift dry ingredients
into a large bowl. Combine applesauce, molasses and oil and add to bowl. Stir
just to combine. Do not beat.

Fill muffin cups about 2/3 full. (A small ladle is a good tool for this.) Bake
about 25 minutes, or until a toothpick tester comes out dry.

Pears In Red Wine

8 firm ripe pears, peeled, cored, stems left on
1 cup sugar, or to taste
3 cups dry red wine
1 stick cinnamon

Bring wine and sugar to boil in a heavy-bottomed saucepan. Add cinnamon stick. Cover and boil over low heat until sugar is dissolved, about 5 minutes. Add the pears and cook them gently over low heat, turning occasionally, until tender, about 10 minutes. (Test by piercing with a sharp, narrow-bladed knife.) Remove cinnamon stick and cool the pears in the syrup, covered.

Using a slotted spoon, remove the pears to a serving dish. Stand them upright and pour the syrup over them. Can be served hot or cold. Makes 8 servings.

Note: Bartlett, Bosc and Anjou are all good for this dish. If you don't have a pot big enough to hold all the pears at once, do them in two batches.

TU B' SHEVAT

Tevet/Shevat

"If you are holding a sapling in your hand when the Messiah comes, first plant the sapling, then go out to greet the Messiah."   Talmud

Menu 1	Menu 2
Walnut-Mushroom Pâté and Crackers	Fattoush Salad
Bulgur Wheat and Parsley Salad	Spaghetti Squash
Vegetarian Chili	Tofu With Cashew Nuts
Orange, Onion and Arugula Salad	over rice
Date Pudding-Cake	Sharon Fruit Gratin Cup
	Carob Chip Cake

Recipes for Tu B'Shevat At A Glance:
Appetizer: Walnut Mushroom Paté
Salads: Bulgur Wheat and Parsley Salad, Grapefruit and Fennel Salad, Fattoush Salad, Orange, Onion and Arugula Salad
Entrées: Vegetarian Chili, Pasta Fruit Fantasia, Tofu and Cashew Nuts
Side Dishes: Sweet Rice Pudding, Couscous with Dried Fruit
Vegetable: Spaghetti Squash
Desserts: Eco Compote, Stuffed Apricots, Date Pudding-Cake, Sharon Fruit Gratin Cup With Brown Sugar and Rum, Carob Chip Cake

Few Jewish holidays so completely convey the meaning of the holiday through specific foods as Tu B'Shevat, which celebrates the birthday of the trees and is also called "the Festival of Fruit." The tree is a dominant metaphor in Jewish literature, beginning with the trees in the Garden of Eden, and continuing with the abiding metaphor of "the tree of life," and the tamarisk tree, the source of manna for the Hebrews in the desert.

Tu B'Shevat became a favorite holiday with the Kabbalists during the Middle Ages and acquired many symbolic meanings which we will explore in the following Tu B'Shevat haggadah. The Kabbalists celebrated the holiday with a formal vegetarian seder. Because of its joyous expression of respect for the tree, Tu B' Shevat has become an important holiday for modern Jews as a symbol of the Environmentalist movement and respect for nature. There are today several Tu B' Shevat haggadot. Some weave elaborate symbols about fruit and trees; some are scholarly or kabbalistic; some sound modern in tone, reminding us of the many environmental concerns voiced in Torah.

For example, a prominent Jewish environmental law concerns the prohibition against cutting down fruit-bearing trees, even in wartime when wood might be necessary for weapons. (Deut. 20:19) This commandment gave rise to the more inclusive commandment of bal tashchit, which forbids us to waste anything or to use nature wantonly. The eminent 19th century rabbi, Samson Raphael Hirsch considered the law of *bal tashchit* as foremost among Jewish values. The prohibition against cutting down fruit trees was later expanded in the Talmud to include a prohibition against the wanton use of food, clothing, furniture and even water. The ecological principle of concern for trees captured the Jewish imagination in the greening of the desert and the rebuilding of Eretz Israel.

Judaism developed many environmental principles, such as prohibitions against smoke, dust, noxious smells and vibrations. Deuteronomy 23:13 lays down laws regarding the disposal of sewage and prohibits the dumping of sewage into rivers or the littering of the countryside. Numbers 35:2 commands open undeveloped space, or a "commons," called a "migrash" in the Bible, which may be the earliest recorded example of town planning.

Jewish environmental ethics stems from the Jewish teaching that there is a Divine plan to creation and that we must regard creation, nature and all that is in nature, as holy. The prayers are meant to remind us that human beings do not create anything, that "the earth is the Lord's" and not ours. We do not own creation. Tu B'Shevat honors the origin of our concern with the environment, the commandment not to cut down fruit trees.

Our God,
we voice our praise for the world You have created,
for the land of our people restored,
for Torah which nourishes our souls.

We now enjoy the fruits of Your world
with words of thanks and songs of joy.

Creator of all worlds, the flow of Your spirit
makes all plants sprout, all trees bud.

We praise You on this day for forming buds
that bring us luscious fruits.

May it be Your will, Adonai our God,
that as we eat this fruit with love for You,
acknowledging Your greatness, singing Your praises,
Your power will cause buds to form,
beautiful blossoms and ripe fruit to grow in abundance
for good and for blessing.

May the Land give its plenty and the trees of the field their fruit.

Foods used in a Tu B'Shevat seder are red wine and white wine, or red juice and a pale juice; almonds, pomegranates, olives, dates, figs and carob. The recipes here are based on foods from trees: coconuts, pineapples, apples, pears, quince, peaches, plums, dates. The Hebrew word for fruit, "pe-ri," also includes nuts, olives and grains. The Tu B'Shevat seder is a ceremony in which we express our thanks to God for these foods. We will therefore eat accordingly, with thanks for the fruit of God's earth:

Historical Background

The festival of Tu B' Shevat, the 15th of Shevat, is one of four First-of-the Year periods, or Rosh Hashanot, contained in every year. Louis Berman's *Haggadah for Tu B' Shevat* observes several interesting Sephardic customs:

"Sephardic Jews call this day Frutas, the Festival of Fruits, or Rosana das Arbores, Rosh Hashana of the Trees. In Morocco, the rich invite the poor to fill their hats with fruit.....In Turkey, a whole-grain pudding called kofyas was served on the eve of Tu B' Shevat, to express the hope for abundant crops in the coming year...parents took their children, each armed with a drawstring bag, on a round of visits to their relatives. At each home, an elaborate table was spread with a variety of nuts and dried fruits, and the children were given treats to take home in their drawstring bags.

"Three blessings were recited by Jews of Turkey in honor of Las Frutas. First, the blessing for wheat, when kofyas is served. Next, the blessing for the fruit of the trees, which called for eating alharubas (carob), manganas (pomegranates), or any available dried fruit. Lastly the fruit of the vine was blessed, by eating grapes or melons."

The other Rosh Hashanot are the 1st of Nisan, which relates to the Kings of Israel and to the pilgrim festivals, the 1st of Elul, which concerns the tithing of animals and sacrificial offerings and, as such, one which no longer applies; and the third is the 1st of Tishrei, which is the familiar Rosh Hashanah on which occurs the judgment of humankind as well as other reckonings. In the Mishnah (Rosh Hashanah 1.1) the 15th of Shevat is designated as Rosh Hashanah la-le-Ilanot. It was the New Year of the Trees and the time for determining the tithes of the fruits of the trees. It forms the boundary between one year and the next, since by then most of the annual rains in Eretz Israel have fallen and the soil has been saturated. Sap has begun to rise in the trees, and trees that are newly planted after the 15th of Shevat are likely to take firm root and produce fruit.

In Deuteronomy 8, the Torah praises the land of Israel.

"...a land of wheat and barley and vines and fig trees and pomegranates...a land of olive trees and honey."

Tu B'Shevat, for hundreds of years, was considered no more than a minor holiday. Yet it continued to receive interest, and to be celebrated. Ashkenazic communities in Europe marked it by the singing of Psalm 104, and the fifteen Psalms of Ascent 120-134, known as Shir Ha Ma'alot. This was accompanied by the eating of 15 kinds of fruit, complementary to the 15 psalms and the 15th of Shevat. Then, in Israel there developed a more elaborate and mystical response. The Kabbalistic community of Safed of the 16th century initiated a yearly practice of holding a Tu B' Shevat seder, replete with both mystical and traditional readings and with ritual, which they patterned on the Passover seder. The special order of that seder is attributed to Nathan of Gaza, and it was called Hemdat Ha-Yamin, "The Loveliness of the Right." Another description of the Kabbalistic seder and its liturgy, expanded to include additional readings, was recorded by the great 17th century mystic, R. Hayyim Vital, and is called *Peri Ez Hadar,* "The Fruit of The Glorious Tree."

From those sources, we have learned that the seder included the blessing and eating of selected fruits from the land of Israel, the drinking of four cups of wine, the reading of excerpts from the Talmud, Midrashic stories, quotations from the Bible and recitation of a special closing prayer. There were also specified readings from the great 13th century mystical text, the Zohar, and from other works.

THE SEDER OF TU B'SHEVAT

Produced by Evelyn Dorfman for The Jewish Vegetarian Society of Toronto,
and reprinted by permission of Evelyn Dorfman

באחד בשבט ראש השנה לאילן כדברי בית שמאי.

בית הלל אומרים בחמשה עשר בו.

(Rosh ha-Shanah 1.1)

Today we celebrate the New Year of the Trees and rejoice together in eating the fruit of the vine and of the tree. Today we reaffirm our bonds with all Creation and with our Creator, with our precious Torah, and with the bond of our people, Israel.

Kaddesh

We sanctify the day with the recitation of Kiddush.

ברוך אתה יי אלהינו מלך העולם בורא פרי הגפן.

Baruch Atah Adonai Elohaynu Melech Ha Olam Borei P'ree Ha-Gafen

Blessed art Thou, Lord our God, Creator of the Universe Who creates the fruit of the vine.

Now, tonight, by the very interest you have shown in being here, and with your participation in the act of sanctified eating, and by your "hearing ear," we remind ourselves of our common heritage as moral creatures of the one God. We pay tribute to our sacred heritage as Jews by celebrating the ever-present benefits of nature with which we are blessed.

It is a great pleasure for us to join together to acknowledge the blessings of nature's yearly renewal, and the gift of good and sweet food from its harvest. We affirm together the privilege of life and the potential of wisdom, through the acceptance of the ever-extending emanation from our Creator.

Urchatz

The Washing of Hands

We begin with the ritual of blessing and drinking the first of four glasses of wine, or grape juice. We celebrate with both the white and the red.

Traditionally, the white symbolizes the time when the sun's rays begin to weaken, on the 15th of Av, and the red recalls that six months later, on the 15th of Shevat, there is an awakening of the soil and the beginnings of growth.

In its mystical reference, the white wine or juice we drink is symbolic of the white, bleak and dry state of the earth in the season of winter. It signifies the pre-spring and re-birth state of creation in which the creative focus is only on life's potential. It is not a dead or inactive condition, but rather a condition of hidden germination.

Please pour some white wine or grape juice into your glass.

Bracha Al Ha Yain

We drink our first cup of white wine.

ברוך אתה יי אלהינו מלך העולם בורא פרי הגפן.

Baruch Atah Adonia Elohaynu Melech Ha Olam Borei P'ree Ha-gafen

Blessed art Thou, Lord our God, Creator of the Universe, who creates the fruit of the vine.

Maggid

The intrinsic structure of the Kabbalistic seder is built on a mystical concept of the Four Worlds. "Each world, corresponding to a different letter of the Divine Name, represents a different level of our being. With each cup of wine we enter into a different world and eat the fruits which correspond to that world. We eat the fruits in ascending order of the worlds, in accordance with the ruling of the school of Hillel regarding the Chanukah lights: "We ascend in holiness, not descend." (Shabbat 21b)

The four worlds are called:

Assiah--the body
Yetzirah---the emotion
Beriah--the mind
Atzilut--the essence of being
(From Simcha Steven Paull, "A Tu B'Shevat Haggadah" "Pri Etz Hadar")

P'ree Ha-Etz

The first kind of fruit we eat is one with a non-edible shell. It is one that must be broken in order to obtain the edible interior. It is symbolic of the lowest of the four worlds--Assiah, and of the kind of human being whose goodness and humanity become accessible through the actions of outside effort and change.

Following the blessing on the fruits, please eat the almonds which we've partially opened for your convenience, and also the fruit of the tough-skinned pomegranates.

Blessing of the fruits:

ברוך אתה יי אלהינו מלך העולם בורא פרי העץ.

Baruch Atah Adonai Elohaynu Melech Ha Olam Borei P'ree Ha-Aytz

Blessed art Thou, Lord our God, Creator of the Universe, Who brings forth the fruit of the tree.

Bracha Al Ha Yain

Our second glass of juice or wine will be a blending of a little bit of red wine or red juice into the white. This is to make a rosy or pale pink effect, reflective of the early growing plants of spring. Please pour a little red wine or juice into the white in your glass.

ברוך אתה יי אלהינו מלך העולם בורא פרי הגפן.
Baruch Atah Adonai Elohaynu Melech Ha Olam Borei P'ree Ha-Gafen

Blessed art Thou, Lord our God, Creator of the Universe, Who creates the fruit of the vine.

Please drink the wine or juice.

"Once when Rav Kook was walking in the fields, lost in deep thought, the young student with him inadvertently plucked a leaf from a branch. Rav Kook was visibly shaken by this act and, turning to his companion, said gently: 'Believe me when I tell you that I never simply pluck a leaf or a blade of grass of any living thing unless I have to. Every part of the vegetable world is singing a song and breathing forth a secret of the divine mystery of the creation.' The words of Rav Kook penetrated deeply into the mind of the young student. For the first time he understood what it means to show compassion to all creatures."　　　(*Wisdom of the Jewish Mystics, p. 80*)

P'ree Ha-Etz

The second type of fruit we eat is formed with a soft exterior and a hard pit center, as there is in dates and olives. It is not unlike those of us who may give the appearance of being open to receive love and communication but who, when tested, lack compassion and have a heart of stone. That level has been interpreted to mean that if such a stone were re-planted either by the human will to change, or through the Kabbalistic conception of re-incarnation, the person could be renewed and his or her intrinsic sparks of holiness could be released.

Let us join in the blessing and eating of the dates and olives.

ברוך אתה יי אלהינו מלך העולם בורא פרי העץ.
Baruch Atah Adonai Elohaynu Melech Ha Olam Borei P'ree Ha-Aytz

Blessed art Thou Lord our God, Creator of the Universe Who brings forth the fruit of the tree.

While the Torah has long referred to God as the Tree of Life, the sages of Safed envisioned the concept of God as being like an inverted tree Whose roots are centered in heaven and Whose trunk and branches extend down toward God's creations, becoming ever more in touch with the world below and with human comprehension. They visualized that reaching out to us from the branches of this Tree were God's emanations or *S'Phirot* which were touching and revitalizing us with God's eternal life.

111

Tu B' Shevat was experienced not only as the New Year of Trees of the Talmud, but even more as the New Year of the Tree, meaning the Tree of Life. To the mystics it was a wondrous time, a time in which the Tree of Life renews its flow of life to the whole universe. "It is," says Arthur Waskow "as if the day were God's own Rosh Hashanah. Just as we need God's presence on our Rosh Hashanah to help us renew our days, so God, as it were, needs our presence on this one."   (Arthur Waskow, *Seasons of Our Joy)*

Our human role or response, the mystics say, is in the eating of the fruits of our earthly vegetation which symbolize the seasons' revitalization through the flow of life. If, when we eat, we hallow the act by saying the proper blessings and by directing our awareness, the life flow is maintained and it is received.

Bracha Al Ha-Yayin

The third glass of wine or juice is a half and half combination of red and white, reminiscent of the full blooming colors of spring and summer. It is a reflection of the warmth and the strength of our own maturity when, in life, we have also been blessed to attain that level.

Please pour your wine or juice of half red and half white.

ברוך אתה יי אלהינו מלך העולם בורא פרי הגפן.

Baruch Atah Adonai Elohaynu Melech Ha Olam Borei P'reee Ha-Gafen

Blessed art Thou, Lord our God, Creator of the Universe Who creates the fruit of the vine.

Please drink the wine or juice.

Yehuda Haezrahi in the book, *Saplings,* describes the meaning of this festival to Jews in the Diaspora.

"In northern climes, where Tu B'Shevat fell on a cold wintry day in February, Jews could look out of frosted window panes and think of a land far away where the sun was shining and trees were beginning to bloom. Jews could symbolize their longing for their land and their eternal attachment to it by observing the custom of eating fruit."

One asks: why is the Torah compared to figs? Most trees such as the olive, grape or date, produce fruit that can be gathered all at one time, but the fig is gathered bit by bit. *(Shir Hashirim Rabba: 4)*

P'ree Ha-Etz

The third type of fruit represents the world of Beriah, and this is the fig. A fig is one of those fruits that is edible both on the inside and the outside. It can be seen as a symbol of that part of humankind which can open its heart and its mind to others. It can attain a direct experience of God's light without an impediment or hard core to hinder such a flow.

ברוך אתה יי אלהינו מלך העולם בורא פרי העץ.

Baruch Atah Adonai Elohaynu Melech Ha Olam Borei P'ree Ha-Aytz

Blessed art Thou, Lord our God, Creator of the Universe Who brings forth the fruit of the tree.

Please eat the figs.

Another fruit that exemplifies this level of total accessibility is the venerable carob, or bokser, which is an ancient staple in Israeli food. It is a particular pleasure for us to eat this fruit for the very first time this season, as it enables us to recite the Shehecheyanu b'racha.

ברוך אתה יי

אלהינו מלך העולם שהחינו וקימנו והגיענו לזמן הזה.

Baruch Atah Adonai Elohaynu Melech Ha-Olam Shehecheyanu V'kiymanu V'higiyanu Lazman Hazeh

Blessed art Thou, Lord our God, Creator of the Universe, Who has kept us alive, preserved us, and kept us until this occasion.

Please eat the carob.

In his essay called Shevat, Rabbi Samson Raphael Hirsch reminds us that when Jewish law reckons the 15th of Shevat as the birthday of the fruits, it also "regulates accordingly the whole series of duties which the annual gifts of nature impose upon the Jew."

"In the Jewish land, where the Divine law has full scope, nothing was supposed to germinate or blossom or ripen without bringing the Jew obligations as well as enjoyment. A duty is attached to every enjoyment, and this gives the enjoyment its true taste by turning what would otherwise be a selfish and subhuman act into a human acknowledgment of Divine love. (p. 35)

It is wonderful how the Jewish law continually
invites us to the observation of the laws and
ways of nature, and how it is ever leading us
from Nature to the life of the human being, there
teaching us to use the products of the soil
for bringing to ripeness the still nobler
blossoms and fruits of a free human life
permeated with the idea of God (p. 36)

Law is the great watch-word
Which in the scheme of the Torah is everywhere
wedded with Jewish freedom, warning us that
freedom is the breath of life or humanity,
but caprice and license stifle it.   (p. 37)
See Leviticus 19.19 and Deuteronomy 22:9

In reference to the law of Maaser, the duties of the apportionment of tithes:

The first tithe belonged to the spirit in Israel.
But a second tithe of almost equal volume belonged
to the body and was devoted to physical consumption,
to pure, gladsome, sensual enjoyment. It was to
be consumed in Jerusalem, in the surroundings of
the Sanctuary, with joy and gladness
Hirsch, Judaism Eternal

Here lies the nerve center of Judaism, here is the kernel of this divine and wonderful creation which is so deeply misunderstood.

It is not in sorrow and sadness, not in self-
castigation and torture that Judaism reaches
its highest level; its holiest goal is serenity,
gladness and joy.
"Not in heaviness of heart and not in pain and not
in despondency," and not in frivolity either does
the Jewish spirit find a lodgment. Where pure and
thoughtful joy dwells, there it dwells too.
Frivolity flees before the earnestness of the
Jewish Law, and the Divine truth of that Law drives

114

away pain and mourning and teaches one to live a
serene, happy life on earth.
The spirit of Judaism knows of no cleavage in human existence
which assigns the spirit of the human being to God
and the body to Satan, by which the earth should belong to hell
and happiness begin only in the celestial beyond.
"Prepare for Me here on earth a holy abode,
so that I may dwell with you already on earth,"
says the spirit of Judaism in the name of God.
It takes the whole human being,
both sensual and spiritual, into its domain,
so that even sensuous enjoyment becomes a holy service
of God when it is inspired with the
Spirit of modesty, temperance and holiness,
and when a human being enjoys the manner
so pure and acceptable to God.
And for such holy and acceptable ends we can raise our eyes
cheerfully and joyfully to God and do not need
to flee from the neighborhood of God's sanctuary.
To be able to abide in the sphere of God with
our physical satisfactions and enjoyments--
this is the highest perfection of the morally-endowed human
upon earth. (p.38-39; Deut. 14:22 and Mishnah Tractate Maaser Sheni)

Bracha Al Ha-Yayin

Our fourth glass is reminiscent of the darkening colors of autumn and of the slowly declining latter stage of life which is the natural evolution for both plants and people.

We pour a glass of fully red wine or juice, but add just a few drops of white. This white intrusion into the full splendor of the red is an indication that we can never attain a state of perfection in this mortal world. Please prepare your glasses with full red and a little white. We do not eat fruit when we relate to the fourth world of Atzilut, because that is a spiritual state beyond any representation.

ברוך אתה יי אלהינו מלך העולם בורא פרי הגפן.

Baruch Atah Adonai Elohaynu Melech Ha Olam Borei P'reee Ha-Gafen

Blessed art Thou Lord our God, Creator of the Universe Who creates the fruit of the vine.

115

There is a Midrash that when God created the world, everything was made a little bit incomplete. Instead of making bread grow out of the earth, wheat was made so that people might make it into bread. Instead of creating earth out of bricks, clay was made so that people might bake the clay into bricks. Why? So that men and women would be partners in the task of completing the work of creation.

P'ree Ha Adamah

Wheat and barley are examples of food that we cannot use as they are in their raw state. They require modification and transformation into a form in which they can be nutritionally absorbed. Some rabbis have seen this as a paradigm for the human condition, teaching us that there are some matters that require our active intervention to bring them forth from their state of potential usefulness to actual usefulness.

We will enjoy two prepared forms of wheat and barley after we commence our seder meal with the Motzi.

Motzi

ברוך אתה יי אלהינו מלך העולם המוציא לחם מן הארץ.

Baruch Atah Adonai Elohaynu Melech Ha-Olam Ha-Motzi Lechem Min Ha-Aretz

Blessed art Thou, Lord our God, Creator of the Universe, Who brings forth bread from the earth.

Shulchan Orech

The Seder Meal

<u>Walnut Mushroom Pâté</u>

1 teaspoon canola oil, spray or vegetable broth
1 medium onion, finely chopped
1/2 pound mushrooms, sliced
2 cups walnuts, toasted
1/2 pound firm tofu, patted dry and crumbled
2 tablespoons nutritional yeast flakes
2 tablespoons tamari

Heat large skillet; add oil, spray or broth. Add onion, brown quickly over medium high heat so that onion stays crisp.

Add mushrooms, cover, cook for 3 minutes. Uncover and cook, stirring occasionally, until mushrooms release their juices, and are lightly browned.

Put mixture into food processor and blend until smooth. Add remaining ingredients; process until smooth. Transfer to serving dish; cover, refrigerate at least 1 hour, preferably more. Spread on crackers or stuff in cherry tomatoes, celery boats, etc. Makes 3 cups.

Note: To toast nuts: place walnuts on baking sheets, bake at 350^0 F. for 10 minutes.

<u>Bulgur Wheat and Parsley Salad</u>

Grain foods should be included in a Tu B'Shevat seder for the kernels of grains are technically fruit, and are regarded as fruit in Jewish tradition.

1 cup bulgur wheat
2 cups boiling water
1/2 cup chopped fresh parsley
Juice of 1/2 lemon
Salt and pepper to taste

Place bulgur in saucepan, pour boiling water over it, cover and let stand for 20 minutes. Mix chopped parsley into the bulgur, pour in lemon juice (adjust the amount of lemon juice to taste.) Add salt and pepper.

Variation: Add 1/2 cup of cooked, drained frozen tiny peas.

Grapefruit and Fennel Salad

Tu B'Shevat is a good time to enjoy this salad, if fennel is available in your area. Use a combination of white, pink and ruby grapefruit for color, echoing the wines we use in the Tu B'Shevat seder.

4 medium grapefruit
4 medium fennel bulbs, trimmed,
      tough outer leaves discarded
6 tablespoons virgin olive oil
Kosher salt and freshly ground pepper to taste

Peel the grapefruits, being careful to cut away all of the white pith. With a serrated knife, slice into rounds about 1/4" thick. If grapefruit are very large, it may be easier to cut them in half and make half-moon slices. Arrange the slices in an attractive pattern on a serving platter or on individual plates.

Remove the root ends of fennel bulbs and cut bulbs in half lengthwise. Cut out the core of each bulb, then make slender match stick strips. Scatter fennel strips on top of fruit. Spoon olive oil over all and season with salt and pepper. Serve at room temperature or chilled. Serves 8.

Note: You can save the feathery leaves at the top of the fennel, chop them and sprinkle them on top for additional color and flavor.

Fattoush Salad

1 green pepper, finely diced
2 large cucumbers, peeled and finely diced
1 large mild onion, coarsely chopped
3/4 cup chopped parsley
1/3 cup chopped mint
1 bunch arugula leaves
1 head romaine lettuce, cut in bite-size pieces
4 cloves garlic, crushed
1/4 cup lemon juice
1/3 cup olive oil
1 tablespoon ground sumac, if available
1/2 teaspoon salt
Freshly ground black pepper
4 tomatoes or 6 plum tomatoes, in 1/2" dice
3 large pitas, split into 2 disks, cut into bite-size pieces

Toast pita bits under the broiler until they are crisp. Watch carefully to make sure they don't burn.

In a large bowl, combine green pepper, cucumber, onion, parsley, mint, arugula and romaine. In a small bowl or screwtop jar, combine garlic, lemon juice, oil, sumac, salt and pepper, pour over salad and toss gently but well. Cover and chill for up to 3 hours.

Fifteen minutes before serving, add the tomatoes and pita bits. Toss the salad again and correct for seasonings. Serves 8.

Note: Proportions are not sacred in this recipe. Also, some people prefer to let the pita bits absorb the juices of the salad and add them at the beginning. Others prefer them crisp as in this version. It's your choice. A good way to use up stale pita.

Orange, Onion and Arugula Salad

Israel has long had a well-deserved reputation for its fine citrus fruits, especially its Jaffa oranges. Moroccan Jews serve a version of this salad on Tu B'Shevat.

6 oranges, peeled and sliced thin
6 tablespoons vegetable oil
2 tablespoons + 1 teaspoon mild wine vinegar
1/4 teaspoon salt
2 tablespoons orange juice
Pinch cumin
1 large red onion, thinly sliced
Large bunch of arugula, stems removed
24 Mediterranean-type black olives: optional garnish

Mix oil, vinegar, salt, orange juice and cumin in a small bowl. Layer orange and onion slices, overlapping, in a non-reactive bowl. Pour on the dressing and marinate at room temperature for at least one hour. Arrange a few arugula leaves on each individual serving plate and top with the salad. Garnish with olives, if desired.

Vegetarian Chili

Chilis have a long list of ingredients which can look intimidating, but they are worth the trouble. They can be prepared in advance, they make good company dishes and they can be served hot or cold. Flavor improves with standing.

1/2 pound tofu, drained well, shredded coarsely and
                                    marinated for one hour
1/4 - 1/2 cup tamari or soy sauce for tofu marinade
1 pound kidney beans, soaked overnight and
    cooked according to directions in appendix on beans
4 tablespoons vegetable oil, divided
1 large onion, diced
1 cup celery, diced
1 medium green pepper, seeded, diced
1 large carrot, grated
1 teaspoon salt
1 teaspoon cumin, or to taste
1/2 teaspoon mustard powder
1/2 teaspoon chili powder, or to taste
1 can tomato sauce
1/4-1/2 cup sherry (optional)

Heat 2 tablespoons oil in 12" skillet. Sauté onions until translucent.
Add celery, green pepper; and cook ten minutes.
Add grated carrots, cook another five minutes.
Add spices, beans, tomato sauce and sherry, cover and cook over low heat two minutes.

Heat 2 tablespoons of oil in a small skillet. Sauté tofu quickly over medium heat for about 5 minutes. When tofu begins to brown, add to chili and mix thoroughly. Cover and cook another 2-4 minutes to heat through thoroughly. Serves 8.

Note: 2 1 pound can of beans, drained, can be used. Frozen and defrosted, marinated tofu gives a crunchy texture to the tofu for this recipe. See **Tips About Tofu.**

Tip: Leftover chili can be used as sauce for spaghetti. Purée if thinner sauce is desired.

Pasta Fruit Fantasia

1 pound box rotelle noodles
Pinch of salt in noodles
1 large can crushed pineapple
2 small cans mandarin orange segments
1/2 teaspoon nutmeg or cinnamon

Cook and drain noodles according to directions on package.
Drain fruits well. Pat dry with kitchen toweling.
When noodles have cooled a bit, add fruit, sprinkle spices lightly on top.
Serve at room temperature or slightly chilled. Serves 8-10.

Variation: If good fresh peaches are available, use instead of one of the other fruits. This pasta dish can be sweet, so it's best not to use more than two fruits. A few fresh green grapes on each serving look wonderful.

Good with a dollop of almond cream on top, sprinkled with nutmeg or cinnamon.

Tofu and Cashew Nuts

Another dish with an Oriental flavor from the Jewish Vegetarian Society of Toronto. This dish is made in 3 stages, but each stage is very quick, as is usual in Oriental dishes, so it is best to have your ingredients prepared. If serving over rice, have your rice prepared.

14 ounces firm tofu, drained
       and pressed dry for 30 minutes
4 tablespoons Teriyaki sauce
1 tablespoon tamari sauce
2 tablespoons honey
Salt and pepper to taste
4-5 scallions
3 tablespoons safflower oil
3 cloves garlic, crushed
3 slices fresh ginger root, chopped finely
Crushed chili pepper to taste (not too strong)
2 cups mushrooms, sliced
3/4 cup unsalted cashew nuts, roasted
2 teaspoons dark sesame oil

Cut the tofu in half horizontally, and then into 1/2" cubes.
Mix together the teriyaki sauce, tamari, honey, salt and pepper in a bowl. Cut scallions into thirds, separating white and green parts. Then cut each piece lengthwise into shreds.

Heat 2 tablespoons of oil in a wok or skillet. Add 2/3 of the garlic and ginger and stir fry for 30 seconds. Add the chilis, the white parts of the scallions and the mushrooms. Stir fry for 2 minutes, then set aside in a bowl.

Heat remaining oil over high heat in the same wok or skillet, and stir-fry remaining garlic and ginger for a few seconds. Add the tofu with the teriyaki sauce mixture, and stir-fry over a medium heat for 3 minutes. Add the mushroom and white scallion mixture and toss in the sauce until well coated.

Stir in the cashew nuts and green scallions. Sprinkle with the sesame oil and serve immediately. Excellent over rice. Serves 6.

Spaghetti Squash

If you haven't tried this vegetable before, you will be amused by its metamorphosis.

One 3 pound squash
margarine, salt and pepper to taste

Heat oven to 350^0 F. Pierce the rind of the squash in about 5 places with the tines of a cooking fork. Bake about 1-1 1/2 hours until tender. Cut the squash in half end to end. Scoop out the seeds and the stringy fibers around them. With a fork, rake the flesh of the squash into spaghetti-like strands. There should be about 5 or 6 cups. Serve with margarine, salt and pepper or a favorite spaghetti sauce. Serves 6-8.

Eco Compôte

An old-fashioned preparation that appeals to modern sensibilities and budgets.

Use 1/2 pound each of two to four different dried fruits. Place in large saucepan; cover with water. Bring water to a low boil and cook five minutes. Turn off heat. Cover the pot and let it sit all day. Add sugar and honey and some fresh lemon juice to taste. You can top with Tofutti ice cream or Rice Dream ice cream, or almond cream for extra richness.

Stuffed Apricots

A Turkish delight from Irma Natan's Sephardic kitchen. Apricots are available in Middle Eastern or international markets.

1/2 pound dried, whole apricots
1 cup sugar
1/2 cup chopped almonds
1/2 cup water
2 tablespoons fresh lemon juice
1 cup cool whip or almond cream
Cookies or cake

Soak dried apricots overnight. Drain, and remove pits. Place apricots in a pot with water, sugar, and lemon juice. Cook over low heat for 30 minutes or until the apricots are soft and water becomes syrupy. Remove from heat and cool.

(Continued)

Open each apricot gently and fill with 1 teaspoon of chopped almonds and 1 teaspoon of cream, and close apricot.

Place each apricot on a round cookie or on a piece of cake. Pour some syrup over it. Serve 2-3 apricots per person---unless, of course, they ask for more.

Sweet Rice Pudding

Wonderful to serve at Tu B' Shevat because you can use a variety of seasonal fruits and nuts.

> 2 cups uncooked short grain rice
> > (should make 4 cups of cooked rice)
> 15 ounce can coconut milk. (vary amount to taste)
> Nutmeg
> Pistachio nuts, chopped and/or whole
> Sliced almonds
> Orange and/or tangerine segments

Cook rice in the usual fashion. Mix with coconut milk. Remove to serving bowl. Sprinkle with nutmeg and garnish with fruits and nuts. Garnishes can be served in small bowls. Use other seasonal fruits as desired.

Variation: Line a deep fluted bowl with the rice pudding, leaving center hollow. Fill center with fruit compote.

Couscous With Dried Fruit

> 2 1/2 cups water
> 2 teaspoons oil
> 2 cups couscous
> 1/4 cup raisins
> 1 1/2 cups dried mixed fruit, finely chopped
> 2 tablespoons honey
> 1/2 cup orange juice
> 2 teaspoons chopped fresh mint

In 2 quart pot, bring water and oil to boil. Remove from heat and stir in couscous. Cover, and let stand 20 minutes. Add raisins, chopped fruit, honey, juice and mint. Fluff up with 2 forks and serve. Serves 8.

Date Pudding-Cake

Everything in life should be as good and as uncomplicated as this cake!

1 teaspoon baking soda
1 cup dates, chopped
2 tablespoons margarine
1 cup boiling water
1 cup flour
1 cup sugar
1 teaspoon vanilla
1 cup nuts, chopped

In medium bowl, sprinkle soda over dates; add margarine to boiling water and pour over dates. Mix flour and sugar and add. Stir in vanilla and nuts.

Preheat oven to 350^0 F.
Spoon batter into an 8" x 8" baking pan. Bake 35 minutes. Serve warm or at room temperature. Serves 8-10.

Sharon Fruit Gratin With Brown Sugar and Rum

Tu B' Shevat is the perfect time to try a new fruit, especially one from Israel. The Sharon fruit is the persimmon that Israeli agriculturists have bred, free of seeds and pucker. Unlike other persimmons, they are sweet when firm or soft and have an edible peel. (They are also known as Fuyu persimmons.) Look for them in your market from about November to mid-March. Try eating them as you would apples, chilled or at room temperature.

8 Sharon fruit
1/2 cup brown sugar
4 tablespoons margarine
1/2 cup finely chopped walnuts or almonds
2/3 cup dark rum or brandy, optional

Cut fruit in half crosswise. Place cut sides up in a lightly oiled shallow baking dish.

In a small bowl, blend sugar, margarine and nuts to form a paste. Spread over the fruit halves.   *(Continued)*

125

Preheat broiler. Broil fruit a few minutes, watching carefully until the tops are bubbly and brown. Pour on the rum and return to oven for 30 to 60 seconds just to heat it.

To serve, arrange on dessert plates and drizzle with the warm rum. Serve immediately. Serves 8.

Carob Chip Cake

2 cups whole wheat flour
1/3 cup carob powder
2 teaspoons baking powder
1/3 cup honey
1/2 cup applesauce
1 cup warm water
1 teaspoon vanilla
1/2 cup chopped walnuts or almonds
1/2 cup carob chips

Preheat oven to 350^0 F.
In a medium bowl, mix first three ingredients together, and set aside.

In a large bowl, mix honey, applesauce, water and vanilla. Add dry ingredients to this mixture and mix well. Fold in chopped nuts and carob chips. Pour into lightly oiled 8" x 8" x 2" baking dish. Bake 35-40 minutes. Serves 8.

Nirtzah

Special Concluding Kabbalistic Prayer
(trans. from Peri Ez Hader, by Joel Moses)

O God, Creator of all the celestial and earthly realm, You have created trees and plants in our world to be an earthly counterpart of their archetypal form above. You created this correspondence of worlds above and below in order to teach humankind the mysteries of existence.

From the living qualities of these fruits, we derive spiritual and physical nourishment. This day of Tu B' Shevat, when trees begin to bud with renewed life, is accompanied by a spiritual renewal in heaven. May it be Thy will, O Lord our God and God of our ancestors, that through the eating of Thy beloved fruits and the mitzvah of saying these blessings, that we may also be blessed with a year of abundance and good health and peace. May all the sparks scattered by us and by our ancestors be gathered to their source and may redemption come to Israel and to the world.

...My people shall build the waste cities and inhabit them; and they shall plant vineyards and drink their wine; and they shall also make gardens and eat their fruit...*Amos 9:14*

Rabbi Tarfon likened the people of Israel to a pile of walnuts. If one walnut is removed, each and every walnut in the pile will be shaken.
Avot DeRabbi Natan 18:1

It was a custom in Beitar that when a boy was born they planted a cedar tree, and when a girl was born, a cypress. At the time of their marriage, they trimmed the branches fom the trees to make a chuppah. *Gittin 57a*

PURIM

Adar

On Purim it is traditional to send children bearing trays of assorted delicacies to neighbors, relatives and friends. This custom, called *Mishloach Manot*, "sending portions," originates in Mordechai's telling the people to commemorate their deliverance from Haman's plot in this way.

(Esther, ch. 9 v. 22)

Select a variety of cookies from the index, arrange them on paper plates, and wrap them attractively, perhaps in colored cellophane.

ESTHER'S BANQUET

Stuffed Mushroom Entrée
Stuffed Eggplant
Stuffed Tomatoes
Van Gogh's Potatoes
Apple Delight
Hamantashen

Recipes for Purim At A Glance:
Stuffed Dish Entrées: Stuffed Mushrooms, Stuffed Eggplant, Stuffed Tomatoes with Rice, à la Grècque
Unstuffed Entrée: Uppuma
Side Dish: Van Gogh's Potatoes
Rice Sauces: Oriental Style Ratatouille, Khoreshe alu
Desserts: Apple Delight, Peach Delight, Hamantashen

Like the Festival of Unleavened Bread, Purim is balanced between the omnipresent threat of destruction and miraculous deliverance. In this case deliverance is carried out through a woman, Esther, in a drama of deliverance which took place in Persia (now Iran) two thousand years ago. In the Purim drama, there is the king of Persia, Ahasuerus; his evil minister, Haman who wishes to destroy the Persian Jews; the king's favorite beloved, Esther; and Esther's indomitable uncle, Mordechai, who urges Esther to denounce Haman to the king. Esther summons the courage to do this, with some help from the wine she serves liberally to Ahasuerus. For this reason, it is customary to drink enough wine until we cannot tell good from evil. It is a holiday celebrated with pageants, parades and ribaldry. Every little girl wants to be Queen Esther. A favorite costume of Israeli boys is the American cowboy's dungarees, boots, ten gallon hat and red kerchief. Many kibbutzim prepare for Purim weeks in advance, sewing costumes and rehearsing plays. Celebrations sometimes go on for two days.

In temple, we read the Megilla, which tells this ancient story and reminds us of the Jewish community which had existed in Persia since the days of the Babylonian captivity and was probably the oldest continuous Jewish community until the recent rise of Islamic Fundamentalism, which caused many Iranian Jews to leave. Many of the great rabbis who wrote the Babylonian Talmud were nourished there.

It is traditional to eat a "stuffed" food or pastry at Purim, such as hamantashen, a pastry filled with mohn or mashed prunes. There are other pastries eaten by Jews around the world at Purim, stuffed with other fillings: turnovers, strudels and kreplakh are made, or stuffed foods such as grape leaves, eggplant, and figs stuffed with nuts. Egyptian Jews make a deep fried pastry that is filled with nuts and honey. Tomatoes and green peppers stuffed with vegetables and grains are appropriate. Many different kinds of foods can be stuffed and many different kinds of stuffings can be made.

It is customary to eat vegetables during Purim, in commemoration of Esther who is said to have eaten vegetables in the king's palace to avoid eating non-kosher food. Since Purim celebrates an event in the Babylonian/Persian Jewish community of two thousand years ago recipes of Persian Jews seem appropriate. Rice is their staple food.

Blessing For Rice

Blessed art Thou Creator of the Universe
Who has created dishes for the delight of all.

Stuffed Mushroom Entrée

Combine different rices for a variety of tastes and textures, or use 1/2 cup of either rice.

    1/4 cup short grain brown rice and
    1/4 cup sweet brown rice
                or 1/2 cup of either rice
    1 cup water
    10 1/2 oz. package soft or silken tofu
    24 stuffing mushrooms, about 1 1/2-2 pounds
    1 tablespoon margarine, divided
    1 tablespoon olive oil divided
    2 ribs celery, minced
    1 clove garlic, pressed
    1 shallot, minced
    5 shitake mushrooms, thinly sliced
    1 teaspoon dried thyme
    1/2 teaspoon dried basil
    1/2 cup chopped pecans
    1/4 cup golden raisins

Preheat oven to 350° F.
Combine water and rice in small pot and bring to boil.
Reduce heat to low and simmer until water is absorbed, about 35-45 minutes.

Place tofu in food processor or blender and process until creamy.
Remove mushroom stems and save for another use.

Heat 1 1/2 teaspoons each of oil and margarine in large skillet over medium heat. Add mushroom caps and cook 1 minute on each side.
Remove mushroom caps and place in lightly oiled baking dish.

Add remaining margarine and oil to pan. Add celery, garlic, shallot and shitakes and cook for a few minutes until mushrooms are soft. Add herbs, nuts, raisins and tofu. Stir well to combine. If necessary, keep warm over lowest heat until rice has finished cooking. Add cooked rice to tofu mixture and stuff mushroom caps. Bake 30 minutes. Serves 6 as a side dish or first course, 4 as an entrée.

Stuffed Eggplant

4 small eggplants, 1/2 to 3/4 pound each, caps removed
Kosher salt
5 tablespoons olive oil, divided
2 medium onions, finely diced
2 cloves garlic, finely chopped
6 medium plum tomatoes, peeled and diced
1 teaspoon dried oregano
1/4 cup dry white wine or water
2 cups cooked rice
2 tablespoons lemon juice
4 teaspoons finely chopped fresh mint
1/4 teaspoon cinnamon
1 teaspoon salt
Freshly ground black pepper
Mint sprigs and lemon wedges for garnish

Cut eggplants in half and salt them generously with kosher salt to draw out any bitter juices. After 30 minutes, scrape off the salt, squeeze gently and rinse.

Remove the eggplant pulp, leaving a shell about 3/8" thick. Reserve the pulp.

Boil 4 or more inches of water in a pot big enough to hold several of the shells at once. Reduce heat, and simmer shells for 5 minutes. Remove and drain upside down on a rack.

In a 10" or 12" skillet, heat 3 tablespoons of olive oil. Add onion and sauté until tender. Add garlic and sauté 1 or 2 minutes longer. Remove onion and garlic with slotted spoon and reserve. Add and heat 2 tablespoons oil, or more if needed. Sauté eggplant until oil is absorbed. Add tomatoes, oregano, reserved onions and garlic, and cook 5 minutes. Stir in wine or water and cover pan. Simmer about 20 minutes, or until vegetables are tender. Stir occasionally, adding liquid if needed.

About half way through simmering time, preheat oven to 400⁰ F.

When vegetables are ready, add rice, lemon juice, cinnamon, mint, salt and pepper. Mix well.

Grease a shallow baking dish and place shells on it. Fill the shells and cover the dish loosely with foil. Bake 10 minutes; uncover, and bake 10 minutes more or until shells are tender when pierced with a sharp knife. If filling *(Continued)* begins to dry out, sprinkle with a little water and replace foil cover. Serve hot or at room temperature, garnish with mint and lemon. Serves 6-8.

Note About Eggplants: Small Italian eggplants are very nice for this dish. Heartier appetites may prefer regular eggplants, which are easier to find and less expensive. The salting procedure not only draws out bitter juices, it also cuts the amount of oil the eggplant will absorb.

To prepare the shells: use a sharp knife to make an outline about 3/8" in from the peel. Score the pulp in 3/4" squares, penetrating to within half an inch from the bottom. Then use a spoon to pop out the cubes of pulp.

Tomatoes Stuffed With Rice, à la Grècque

8 large firm tomatoes
2 teaspoons salt, or less to taste, divided
Freshly ground black pepper
1/3 cup olive oil, divided
1 cup chopped onions
1/2 cup raw rice
2 tablespoons currants or seedless raisins
1 cup boiling water
2 tablespoons minced parsley
1/4 cup pine nuts
1/2 cup fine dry bread crumbs

Cut a 1/2" slice off stem end of each tomato; reserve the slices. Scoop out as much of the pulp as possible. Sprinkle the tomato shells with half the salt and pepper. Chop and reserve the pulp.

In a 10" skillet, heat 2 or 3 tablespoons of oil; add onions and sauté until golden. Add rice and stir until coated. Add tomato pulp, currants and the rest of the salt and pepper. Add boiling water and stir well. Cover and cook over low heat 10 minutes. Mix in parsley and nuts; taste for seasoning.

Preheat oven to 350⁰ F.
Stuff tomatoes loosely. Oil a shallow baking dish and arrange tomatoes in it, sprinkle with bread crumbs. Bake 45 minutes. Serve hot or at room temperature. Serves 4-6 as a main course, 8 as a vegetable.

Tip: if you have more filling than the tomatoes can hold, place remainder in an oiled dish, top with reserved tomato slices. Brush with oil, sprinkle with crumbs and bake 25 minutes. Good for second helpings.

__Uppuma__ (Pronounced "oopoomah")
With Permission of The North American Vegetarian Society

In the 19th century, under the British Raj, many Iraqi Jews settled in India, chiefly in Bombay and Calcutta, where earlier Jewish groups, the Cochins and Bene Israel, were long established.

In *The Kosher Gourmet,* edited by Batia Plotch and Patricia Cone, Florence Silliman, who was born into the Iraqi-Indian community in Calcutta, gives a description of the lifestyle and foodways she knew as a child. A cooking teacher and a former caterer, she notes that when the first Jewish settlers arrived from the Middle East, "it wasn't long before the traditional (Sephardic) dishes were spiced with more than a hundred Indian flavoring ingredients--chilis, ginger, turmeric, fennel, mustard seeds, coriander, tamarind, cardamom, and lime among them." And so a unique cuisine was born as, once again, Jewish cooks adapted to the local food supply and customs.

Turmeric gives this dish its rich golden color and, with the mustard seeds, its Indian identity. While rice is the basis for much of India's cooking, wheat dominates in the Northern regions. If you are fond of fiery foods, you may have already discovered some of the excellent dishes Indian cuisine offers the vegetarian. Serve this dish in a bowl that sets off its beautiful hue; terra cotta would be a fine choice.

> 2 tablespoons of oil
> 1 teaspoon mustard seeds
> 2 medium onions, diced
> 1 green pepper, seeded, deribbed, diced
> 2 cups bulgur or cracked wheat
> 4 cups hot water
> 1/2 teaspoon turmeric
> 1/2 teaspoon salt
> 2 tablespoons soy sauce
> 1 tablespoon shredded fresh ginger
> 1 cup coarsely chopped cashews or peanuts

Heat oil in heavy 10" skillet. When oil is hot, add mustard seeds. Put lid on for a few seconds while seeds pop. Add onions and peppers. Sauté until tender. Add bulgur or cracked wheat, mixing to coat the grains before slowly adding the hot water. Lower heat and add remaining ingredients except nuts. Stir occasionally, cook about 20 minutes or until the water is absorbed. If grain is not tender, add a little more water and cook a little longer.

When ready to serve, mix in nuts. Serves 10-12.

Van Gogh's Potatoes

This delectable recipe recalls other Jewish communities which prospered and disappeared. Jews had a long history in Provence where they lived comfortably from the first century C.E. There was a Jewish kingdom under Charlemagne. From the beginning of the fourteenth century to the end of the eighteenth the Jewish community in Provence thrived under papal protection.

This recipe was originally called Potatoes à la Provencale and was renamed in honor of Van Gogh, even though his Potato Eaters were surely not eating anything this rich and delicious.

6 tablespoons olive oil
1 cup finely chopped onion
2 cloves garlic, chopped
4 cups potatoes, peeled and cut in large chunks
Dash of grated nutmeg
Salt and pepper
2" strip of lemon peel
Juice of half a lemon (1-2 tablespoons)

In a heavy bottomed 2 or 3 quart pot, warm the oil slightly. Add onions and garlic and stir gently. Add potatoes, seasonings, and lemon peel. Cover and cook over very low heat for 15 minutes. Stir. Cover and continue cooking till potatoes are tender.

With a slotted spoon, remove potatoes from pot and keep them warm. Stir lemon juice into pot, and scrape up any browned bits with a wooden spoon. Heat the juice for a minute or two, then pour over potatoes. Serves 6-8.

Oriental Style Ratatouille

A delicious sauce from the Jewish Vegetarian Society of Toronto, to serve over white rice.

6 tablespoons olive oil, divided
1 small onion, finely chopped
2 cloves garlic, crushed
2 cups canned tomatoes
2 tablespoons tamari sauce
5 tablespoons rice vinegar
Salt and pepper
Chili pepper to taste (not too strong)
2 tablespoons coriander seeds
1 small eggplant cut into 3/4" chunks
1 1/2 cups sliced mushrooms
2 small zucchini, cut in 1/2" diagonal slices
1 yellow and 1 red pepper, cored, seeded, and sliced
2 teaspoons sesame seeds, toasted

Heat 2 tablespoons of oil in a saucepan. Gently sauté onion for 5 minutes until soft. Add garlic, and sauté for 30 seconds. Stir in tomatoes, tamari, and rice vinegar. Add chili pepper and coriander seeds. Season with salt and pepper. Simmer over low heat, stirring occasionally. Sauce should reduce and thicken slightly.

Heat remaining oil in a large skillet, and stir fry eggplant, mushrooms, zucchini and peppers for 5-7 minutes. Add more oil, if necessary. Stir in tomato sauce mixture. Cover and simmer for 10 minutes. Season to taste, and stir in sesame seeds. Serve over white rice. Serves 6.

Prune Sauce (Khoreshe Alu)

When Roberta's friend, Anne Burton, went to Persia on her honeymoon several decades ago, she had the wonderful opportunity of sharing Shabbat dinners with Jewish families who introduced her to Persian dishes used by the Jewish community there. *Khoresh* is a standard sauce used over rice dishes. It can be combined with a variety of foods: fresh or dried vegetables, or fruits, nuts or cereals, depending upon the season and availability of ingredients. It can be made with eggplant, spinach or mushrooms, peas, green plums or sour cherries, quinces, tart apples, or pumpkins. *(Continued)*

When rice is served with a sauce or *khoresh,* it is called *Chelo Khoresh.* It is the favorite dish of Persians and is served every day, and sometimes more often than that. The Persian cook has to use ingenuity to make this dish interesting 365 days a year, and does.

Almost all the *khoreshes* are made the same way, but the seasonings and ingredients vary enormously, and often include meat. The following khoreshes have been adapted for vegetarians.

In Persia, or Iran, your grandmother will feed you *khoreshe alu* or prune sauce when you're not feeling well, but eat this dish at any time.

> 2 tablespoons margarine or vegetable oil
> 1 large onion, minced
> 1 teaspoon salt
> 1/4 teaspoon nutmeg
> 1/4 teaspoon cinnamon
> 2 cups water
> 1/2 tablespoon lemon juice
> 20-25 pitted, dried prunes, soaked overnight
> and drained

Melt margarine in 2 quart sauce pan. Add onions and seasoning. Sauté onions over medium heat, until translucent. Add water and lemon juice. Simmer on low heat, covered, for 10 minutes.

Add prunes to onions and seasonings. Simmer for 20-25 minutes, until prunes are soft. Serve over rice.

Apple Delight

Persians are very fond of desserts made from fruit. Here is a use of apples that is both exotic and practical, since it can be made in advance.

> 4 medium Cortland apples
> 2 tablespoons lemon juice
> 5 tablespoons sugar
> 2 tablespoons rose water
> Crushed ice

Peel apples and grate. Sprinkle with lemon juice to prevent them from darkening. Add sugar and rose water. Stir lightly. Refrigerate for a few hours. Before serving, arrange over a layer of crushed ice. Serves 4-5.

Peach Dessert (Desere Holu)

4 peaches, medium ripe, peeled, sliced
Rose water or cardomom to taste

In a small sauce pan, bring water to boiling. Add peaches. Simmer for 5 minutes. Cool. Just before serving, sprinkle with rose water or dust with cardamom. Serves 4-5.

Variations: Add a dollop of tofu cream, or a few drops of liqueur, or both.

Hamantashen

Kids will love shaping these little goodies, especially since they can put them on the *shalach manot* tray and tell everyone how they helped.

2/3 cups shortening
1/2 cup sugar
1/2 cup mashed ripe banana (about 1 banana)
2-3 tablespoons water
1/2 teaspoon vanilla
2 1/2-3 cups flour
1 recipe filling (recipe follows)

In a large mixing bowl, cream the shortening and sugar. Blend in the banana until smooth. Add the water and vanilla. Stir in the flour gradually, until it is thoroughly integrated and the dough can easily be formed in a ball. Wrap the dough in waxed paper or plastic wrap and chill at least 2 hours. (Overnight is fine and often convenient.)

Preheat oven to 375^0 F.
Divide the dough in quarters and return 3 of them to the refrigerator while the first batch is shaped.

Roll the dough out to about 1/8" thickness. Cut in circles, reflouring utensils as needed. Put a heaping teaspoonful of filling in the center of each circle. Bring up the 3 sides, pinching them together to make three-cornered-hat shapes. Do not close them completely. Filling should show.

Repeat with remaining dough. Bake for 10-15 minutes until the hamantashen begin to brown. Cool on racks. Makes about 36.   *(Continued)*

Apple Filling:

2 cups very finely chopped apple
(about 2 medium apples)
2 tablespoons chopped walnuts
1 tablespoon sugar
mixed with 1/4-1/2 teaspoon cinnamon

Mix ingredients all together in a small bowl.
The apples visible in the center of the baked hamantashen may not look cooked, but they are.

Notes: You can use 2 cookie sheets and bake all the hamantashen at once. If you do this, switch their oven positions halfway through baking time. Or you can form half the hamantashen, bake them on one sheet, and form the others while the first batch bakes. Set the unbaked pastries on plates until ready to transfer to sheets.

Variations: Use thick apricot jam as filling. Commercial fillings in poppyseed, prune and apricot can be improved with lemon juice and rind to taste.

HAG HA MATZOT

Nisan

The seder table should be set with wine (or grape juice) for everyone, a cup of wine for Elijah, a plate with three matzot, covered, the seder plate with greens, bitter herbs, and charoset. *Haggadah for The Liberated Lamb* and *Haggadah For The Vegetarian Family* replace the shank bone with olives, grapes, and unfermented grains, based on the passage in Deuteronomy 24:20-25:4, which commands the second shaking of the olive trees and grape vines to be left for the poor, and not to muzzle the ox when he treads out the grain in the fields; and regards these commandments as mitzvot of compassion for oppressed creatures. Some families replace the shank bone and the roasted egg with papier maché models. There should be bowls of salted water within reach of all the guests, candles, flowers, and haggadot.

Seder 1	*Seder 2*
Mock Kishke	Creamy Carrot Soup
Vegetable Medley	Vegetable Nut Loaf
Potato-Garlic Casserole	Curried Fruit
Grated Carrot Vinaigrette	Baked Diced Potatoes
Mushroom Salad	Cucumber Salad
Strawberry-Rhubarb Compote	Chocolate Matzoh Roll,
	with Fresh Berry Garnish

Recipes For Hag Ha Matzot At A Glance:
Appetizer: Stuffed Kishke
Soup: Creamy Carrot Soup
Entrées: Multi-National Potato Casserole, Vegetable Medley, Vegetable Nut Loaf, Roasted Veggie Pizza, Fasta-Than-Pasta-Farfel Bake
Vegetables: Oven-Roasted Potatoes, Potato and Garlic Casserole, Baked Diced Potatoes
Salads: Mushroom Salad, Cucumber Salad, Grated Carrot Vinaigrette; Beet, Carrot and Cabbage Medley
Desserts: No-Bake Chocolate Matzoh Roll with Berry Garnish, Elegant Curried Fruit, Strawberry-Rhubarb Compote, Prune Treats

From its inception Pesach was regarded as the Festival of Unleavened Bread, or Hag ha matzot.

"Remember this day on which you went free from Egypt, the house of bondage, how the Lord freed you from it with a mighty Hand: no leavened bread shall be eaten. You go free on this day, in the month of Nisan. So, when the Lord has brought you into the land of the Canaanites, the Hittites, the Amorites, the Hivites, and the Jebusites, which the Lord swore to your fathers to give you, a land flowing with milk and honey, you shall observe in this month the following practice:

"Seven days you shall eat unleavened bread, and on the seventh day there shall be a festival of the Lord. Throughout the seven days unleavened bread shall be eaten; no leavened bread shall be found with you, and no leaven shall be found in all your territory. And you shall explain this to your child on that day, 'It is because of what the Lord did for me when I went free from Egypt.'" Exodus 13:3-8

In Joshua V there is a lovely description of the first Passover celebrated by the Hebrews in The Promised Land . "...and they ate of the produce of the land on the morrow of the Passover, unleavened cakes and parched corn...."

The history and symbolism of unleavened bread predates the Hebrew nation. It was the common bread of nomadic tribes in the Middle East, and defined the nomad as much as potatoes defined the lower classes in recent times. According to John Cooper the word "matzoh" derives from the Assyrian "massartu." In old Babylonia, ma-as-sa-ar-tum always meant barley, and barley was the principle cereal used to make bread in the ancient world. The Greek word for barley is "moza." The Egyptians are credited with having discovered the properties of yeast, but because risen bread takes time and special conditions to bake properly, risen bread became associated with the settled or city life which the nomad scorned. It has been suggested that the reason the Hebrews took unleavened bread with them is because it was practical to do so. However, the symbolism of unleavened bread is unquestionable: that it was the bread of poor people, of a servant class, of nomads.

Oded Schwartz writes that the original meaning for "Passover" was not a reference to the "passing over" of the angel of death on the night the Hebrews prepared to leave Egypt, but to the "leaping, skipping or gamboling of newborn ewes and lambs." (p. 29) It is a good time to remember that we celebrate the birth of new creatures. The Festival of Unleavened Bread begins on the night of the full moon of the vernal equinox.

On the first day of Hag ha Matzot, at Musaf, the prayer for dew is chanted after the Amidah. This portion is called "Tal."

Dew, precious dew, unto Your land forlorn,
Pour out our blessing in Your exultation,
To strengthen us with ample wine and corn,
And give Your chosen city safe foundation
In dew.

Dew, precious dew, the good year's crown, we wait,
That earth in pride and glory be fruited,
And that the city once so desolate
Into a gleaming crown may be transmuted
by dew.

Dew, precious dew, let it fall upon the land;
From heaven's treasury be this accorded;
So shall the darkness by a beam be spanned,
The faithful of Your vineyard be rewarded
With dew.

Dew, precious dew, to make the mountains sweet,
The savor of your excellence recalling,
Deliver us from exile, we entreat,
So may we sing Your praises, softly falling
Like the dew.

Hag ha Matzot challenges the cook to create dishes for seven days that have no leaven in them. Over the years, Jews have become adept at doing this and have discovered more and more dishes and foods that meet the requirements. Once cakes were limited to honey cakes and nut tortes. Now Jewish bakeries are filled with delights and Sephardic recipes have enriched the Ashkenazi table. Creating vegetarian dishes for the Festival of Freedom is one more challenge that enriches our culinary tradition.

The center piece on the seder table is the seder plate with greens, bitter herbs and charoset. Jewish vegetarians replace the shank bone with a variety of foods: some use a mushroom or a beet.

141

Of all the foods on the seder plate, charoset has captured the culinary imagination, perhaps because its ingredients have lovely associations, as the following passage from the *Shulkhan Aruch* testifies and also demonstrates how highly symbolic Jewish food can be:

"It is proper to prepare the charoset out of fruits to which the people of Israel are likened--for instance, figs, because it is written:

"The fig-tree perfumeth its green figs (*Song of Songs*, 2:13); nuts, because it is said 'into the nut-garden I had gone down (*Song of Songs*, 6:1); 'dates because it is said, "I wish to climb up the palm-tree' (*Song of Songs* 7:9), pomegranates, because it is said, 'Like half the pomegranate' (*Song of Songs* 6:7). Apples, in commemoration of what is said: 'Under the apple tree have I waked thee' (*Song of Songs*, 8:5)...and almonds, because the Holy One, blessed be He, was anxious to bring about their redemption.

"One should put therein spices resembling straw, such as cinnamon and ginger which cannot be ground well and contain some threads resembling straw, in commemoration of the straw they were accustomed to knead into clay."

Jewish communities around the world have created numerous recipes for charoset. There is a tradition for charoset which is made from every fruit mentioned in the Song of Songs. Sephardic charoset often includes figs, dates, and raisins rather than apples. Elsewhere, whatever was grown locally, was plentiful or prized, went into the charoset. Some charoset is raw, some cooked. All have in common that they remind us of the mortar used by Jews when we were slaves in Egypt.

Recently the program committee for Temple Emanu-El Sisterhood in Marblehead researched the subject and prepared many different versions for a unique and successful pre-Passover meeting. The following is the beloved charoset that appears on most American seder tables. You could also try constructing your own according to the above ideas from the *Shulchan Aruch*. You might start a new family tradition.

Charoset

3 apples, peeled, cut in large chunks
1/3 cup chopped walnuts or almonds
1/4 teaspoon cinnamon
1-2 tablespoons sugar
1-2 tablespoons kiddush wine

In food processor fitted with steel blade, combine apples and nuts and process until finely ground. Scrape into a bowl and add cinnamon and sugar to taste. Add enough wine to make a paste, or whatever consistency you prefer. Serves 8-12.

Note: Some families like to make the charoset a few days in advance to let the flavors ripen. You may also want to double the amount and enjoy the leftovers for dessert or snacks.

Stuffed Kishke

8 ounces matzoh meal (about 1 3/4 cups)
1 medium onion, grated fine
1 large carrot, grated fine
3/4 teaspoon salt, or to taste
1/4 teaspoon pepper, or to taste
1 large celery rib, grated fine
4 tablespoons melted margarine

Preheat oven to 350^0 F.
Mix ingredients together and shape into 2 long rolls, each about 2 " in diameter. Grease 2 pieces of foil; place rolls on foil and wrap tightly, but don't squeeze. Place rolls on baking sheet. Bake 1 hour. Open foil and bake another 15 minutes, to brown. Cool slightly before slicing.

May be made in advance and served cold. To reheat, lightly cover rolls with foil and place in oven for about 10 minutes. Can be reheated in microwave. Cut into 2" pieces. Serves 8. Recipe can be doubled.

Creamy Carrot Soup

1 1/2 pounds carrots (about 5 cups), peeled and chopped
2 medium onions, chopped
4 tablespoons oil
12 cups water or vegetable stock
Salt and pepper to taste
2/3 cup parsley, finely chopped

Heat oil in a 6 quart soup pot. Add carrots and onions and sauté over medium heat for 10 minutes or until onions are softened. Add water or stock and seasonings. Bring to boil. reduce heat, cover and simmer   *(Continued)*

20 minutes, or until carrots are tender. Purée in blender and reheat. Serve garnished with chopped parsley. Serves 12.

Variation: Add a dash or two of ground ginger.

Vegetable Medley

1 large eggplant, peeled and chopped
1 red pepper, seeded and chopped
1 green pepper, seeded and chopped
1 onion, finely chopped
1 clove garlic, finely chopped
2 carrots, grated
2 zucchini, peeled and chopped
2 ribs of celery, chopped
1/2 cup Italian style canned tomatoes,
    seeded and chopped
2 tablespoons chopped parsley leaves
1 teaspoon each of salt and pepper
2 pinches each of dried dill, oregano and basil
1 tablespoon red wine vinegar
2/3 cup virgin olive oil
6 medium size potatoes, peeled and diced
(1 cup cooked white or brown rice may be subsituted for
    the potatoes for those who wish)

Heat oil in a large skillet. Sauté onions 5 minutes. Add garlic, peppers, celery, carrots, zucchini, eggplant and tomatoes. Sauté all the vegetables together. Add herbs and cooked rice.

Cook covered over low heat until vegetables are soft.
Add vinegar, salt, pepper.
Uncover and cook until all liquid evaporates, stirring occasionally.

Serve warm as a vegetable, or refrigerate and serve as a dip. Serves 8.

Multi-National Potato Casserole

An Iranian-born Jewish woman of Kurdish-Iraqi descent taught the original version of this dish to her Ashkenazic daughter-in-law from Chelsea, MA., who changed it to suit her cooking style. (The original version was made in individual deep-fried portions.) We adapted it further for the vegan kitchen and are very happy with the results, and with the idea that it is, in its way, a microcosm of Jewish culinary history. This dish is also appropriate for Purim.

> 2 tablespoons oil
> 4 cups sliced mushrooms (about 1 pound)
> 2 cups chopped onions
> 1/2 cup slivered almonds
> 1/2 cup golden raisins
> Salt and pepper
> 8 medium red skin potatoes, boiled and peeled
> 2 teaspoons ground cumin
> 1/2 teaspoon ground turmeric
> 1-3 tablespoons warm water, stock,
> or reserved potato cooking water
> 2 tablespoons margarine, melted

Heat 2 tablespoons oil in 10 " or 12" skillet. Sauté onions and mushrooms until onions are tender and mushrooms give up their liquid. (You may need to cover the skillet for part of the cooking time, especially if you are using a 10" skillet.) Add raisins, almonds, and a sprinkling of salt.

Preheat oven to 375^0 F. Oil an 8 cup casserole, about 7" x 11", or 8" x 8".

Mash potatoes, adding 1 tablespoon or more of warm liquid if necessary to make them workable. Season with cumin, turmeric, salt and pepper, and add most of the melted margarine.

Place a layer of mashed potatoes in the bottom of casserole. Cover it with mushroom mixture. Top with the rest of the potatoes, and brush with remaining margarine. Bake for about 40 minutes. Serves 8.

Variation: If you do not want to use cumin, flavor potatoes with a small chopped onion sautéed in melted margarine or oil. Use turmeric for its rich golden color.

Vegetable Nut Loaf

This dish was adapted from Rose Friedman's *Jewish Vegetarian Cooking.* Can be made early in the day and popped into the oven in late afternoon. The trick to this loaf is to baste it and keep it moist. Use whatever nuts you prefer.

> 1 large onion, finely chopped
> 3 cloves of garlic, finely chopped
> 2 large carrots, grated
> 3 cups of mixed ground nuts
> 1 cup matzoh meal
> 4 tablespoons tomato paste
> 1 large onion, sliced thinly
> 2-1/2 cups vegetable stock

Preheat oven to 350^0 F.
Mix all ingredients, except vegetable stock and sliced onion.

Grease ovenproof casserole; place sliced onions all over the bottom.
Form nut and carrot mixture into a loaf and place on top of sliced onions. Bake 45 minutes. Baste with vegetable stock every 20 minutes. Remove from oven and let cool for ten minutes. Serves 8.

Note: Ingredients can be cut in half for a smaller loaf, but don't worry about having too much: tastes good the next day if left at room temperature.

Oven Roasted Potatoes

> 1 medium size potato per person
> 3 tablespoons olive oil
> Tarragon, oregano, rosemary
>   or paprika to cover potatoes lightly
> Salt

Preheat oven to 400^0 F.
Oil a cookie tin liberally (but not too liberally).
Cut potatoes into large cubes, salt lightly, sprinkle with spice or herb, to taste. Place in baking sheet and turn to cover with oil. Bake for about 1 hour, turn once or twice to make sure potatoes brown evenly.

Variation: Halfway through cooking time, add zucchini, cut into 2" chunks. The combination of potatoes and zucchini is attractive and delicious.

Potato and Garlic Casserole

Another easy potato dish for the seder. If made early in the day, keep at room temperature until 10 minutes before serving. Reheat, uncovered, in oven at 350^0 F.

2 small red potatoes per person, scrubbed, left whole
1 garlic clove for every two potatoes
1/4 cup olive oil
Salt and pepper to taste
Paprika
Tarragon or rosemary to taste

Preheat oven to 350^0 F.
Place potatoes in oven casserole just big enough to hold them in a single layer. Roll in oil to cover. Spread whole garlic cloves between potatoes. Sprinkle salt, pepper and spices to taste. Pour olive oil on top. Cover and bake 50 minutes to 1 hour. If necessary, pop in the oven to reheat, uncovered, 10 minutes before serving.

Baked Diced Potatoes

8 cups peeled, diced potatoes (about 6 medium large)
4 tablespoons oil
1/3 cup minced onion
1 cup minced celery
1/4 cup minced parsley
1 1/2 teaspoons salt
1/4 teaspoon freshly ground black pepper

Place potatoes in 3 quart pot. Cover with cold water; bring to boil. Reduce heat and simmer 5 minutes; drain.

Preheat oven to 375^0 F.
Mix potatoes with remaining ingredients.
Oil a large, shallow baking dish and put potatoes in it. Bake 30 minutes or until the potatoes are golden and just beginning to brown. Serves 8.

Roasted Veggie Pizza

Here's an unusual dish for the holiday. The recipe is time-consuming, but worth it for those days when you're looking for an unusual Passover dinner. The recipe was adapted by Mimi Golfman-Clark from *Eating Well.*

2 cloves garlic, minced
3 cups thinly sliced red onion
1/2 cup water
1/4 cup balsamic vinegar
1 tablespoon maple syrup
1 teaspoon thyme, divided
1/2 teaspoon sea salt
1 red bell pepper, roasted and cut into thin strips
1 yellow bell pepper, roasted* and cut into thin strips
4 fresh basil leaves, slivered
1/2 teaspoon dried rosemary
1/2 teaspoon dried oregano

Matzoh meal to sprinkle on peel, stone or pan
Prepared potato pizza base: see below

Preheat pizza baking stone (if using) in 500^0 F oven.

In a large saucepan, place garlic, onions, water, vinegar, maple syrup, 1/2 teaspoon thyme and salt.

Cook, covered on low heat, stirring frequently 45-60 minutes until liquid evaporates and onions are slightly caramelized; cool. (This mixture can be made in advance and refrigerated.)

Distribute onion mixture over baked potato crust. Scatter peppers over onions. Sprinkle rosemary, oregano and 1/2 teaspoon thyme on top.
Bake 10-15 minutes. Serves 6.

To roast peppers: wash and dry peppers. Place on a cookie sheet about 4" under the heat of a broiler. (You can use a stovetop grill or gas burner, but these can be messy) Char the peppers on all sides until the skins blacken.

Transfer peppers to a paper bag (or covered bowl); close bag allowing peppers to steam for 15 minutes. Rub off charred skin under cool water; seed, derib, and cut into strips. Can be done ahead.

Potato Crust Base

(From Rose Friedman, Jewish Vegetarian Cooking,)

> 1 1/4 pounds potatoes, boiled or steamed and cooled
> 1 tablespoon margarine
> 3/4-1 cup matzoh meal
> 1/4 cup potato flour
> 1/2 teaspoon sea salt

Mash potatoes. Add margarine.

Mix in matzoh meal, potato flour and salt; process or knead by hand until dough forms a ball. If dough is too stiff, add a few drops of water; if dough is too "pasty" gradually add more matzoh meal.

Wrap dough in plastic wrap and refrigerate at least one hour. (Dough may be made the day before; take out of refrigerator and leave at room temperature to soften a bit.)

Lightly spray 2 pans. 7" x 11" or one 12" pizza pan. Roll the dough to fit the pan(s). Bake 20 minutes, until crusty and browned. Top with vegetables.

Fasta-Than-Pasta Tomato Farfel Bake

Easy and delicious for a chol-hamoed meal. You can put it together in 5 minutes, and it will be ready by the time you make a salad and set the table. It comes out of the oven tasting like pasta with a light tomato sauce, and has a similar nutritional value. Reheated, it tastes like scalloped tomatoes. Fine either way.

> 2 1/2 cups crushed, peeled, unsalted, canned tomatoes
> 1/4 cup chopped onion
> 1/2 teaspoon salt
> 1/4 teaspoon pepper
> 1 tablespoon sugar
> 1 1/2 cups matzoh farfel
> 1/4 cup oil

Preheat oven to 375º F.

In a medium bowl, combine tomatoes, onion, salt, pepper and sugar.

In another bowl, mix farfel and oil.

Oil a 1 quart baking dish. Put a layer of the farfel mixture in the bottom of the dish, then a layer of tomatoes.

Repeat, ending with farfel.

Bake 30 minutes or until lightly browned. Serves 6.

Mushroom Salad

The chives that struggle up through the late winter snow by the kitchen door are harbingers of spring and all its freedom, so we like to include them in the seder menu. Here they add a touch of spring to a dish that is good at any season.

> 1 pound mushrooms, cleaned, trimmed and sliced
> Scant 1/2 cup olive oil
> 3 tablespoons vinegar
> 1/2 teaspoon salt
> 1 clove garlic, minced
> 1 tablespoon minced fresh parsley
> 2 tablespoons grated onion
> 1 tablespoon fresh chives, minced
> 1/8 teaspoon dried thyme
> 1/8 teaspoon freshly ground black pepper

Combine all ingredients in glass or ceramic bowl. Marinate 2 hours or longer. Stir salad occasionally. Serves 6-8.

To serve as a first course, present the salad on individual portions of shredded romaine lettuce and garnish with cherry tomatoes. Can also be served as a side dish from a shallow serving bowl.

This marinade is also good for lightly steamed asparagus or green beans, cut into 2" pieces.

Cucumber Salad

Crisp, refreshing and tart, this dish is a good balance for the heartier dishes we enjoy at the seder.

> 3 medium cucumbers, peeled and sliced paper thin
> 1 tablespoon salt
> 2 tablespoons sugar
> 3/4 teaspoon pepper
> 2 tablespoons minced parsley
> 1 teaspoon chopped fresh dill or 1 teaspoon dried
> 1 cup cider vinegar

Place cucumber slices in medium bowl, sprinkle with salt.
Cover with a plate small enough to press down over the cucumbers.
After 1 hour, drain liquid from cucumbers.

Combine remaining ingredients and mix well. Taste and add more sugar, salt, etc., as needed. Mix with cucumbers. Allow to stand several hours. Serves 6.

Carrot Salad With Fresh Ginger

Carrot salads bring a welcome burst of color to the table. This one brings a surprising burst of flavor, too.

> 1 pound carrots, peeled and grated
> 3 tablespoons vegetable oil
> 1 tablespoon fresh lemon juice
> 2 teaspoons finely chopped fresh ginger
> 1/2 teaspoon salt
> Freshly ground black pepper

Combine oil, lemon juice, ginger, salt and pepper in a small screwtop jar. Shake well. Toss with carrots just before serving. Serves 6.

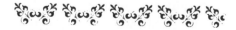

Beet, Cabbage and Carrot Salad

For a striking presentation of this unusual salad, toss each vegetable in the dressing separately. (Use about 1/2 cup on the beets, and a 1/4 cup each on the carrots and cabbage.) On a round serving platter, arrange the beets in a wide border, then make a circle of the cabbage and fill in the center with the carrots.

2 pounds small beets, peeled and grated
2 cups shredded red cabbage
1 cup shredded carrots
1/2 cup lemon juice
1/4 cup honey
1/4 cup vegetable oil
Salt to taste

Combine beets, cabbage and carrots in a large bowl. Whisk together lemon juice, honey, oil and salt. Dress the salad, cover it, and chill. Serves 8.

No-Bake Chocolate Matzoh Roll

This was a longtime favorite in Israel where, in the early decades, not every home had an oven. This dessert is becoming popular here. Everyone who tastes it loves it.

4 squares plain matzoh
Water for moistening matzoh
1/4 cup sugar
3 tablespoons strong coffee
4 ounces semi-sweet chocolate
1 tablespoon brandy, optional
1 cup margarine at room temperature
3/4 cup chopped walnuts

Glaze:
2 ounces semi-sweet chocolate
3 tablespoons water

Garnish:
1 pint strawberries, washed but not hulled

In a large bowl, soak matzoh in water briefly. Drain water and crumble matzoh.

Melt chocolate with coffee and sugar in the top of a double boiler or in a small bowl in a microwave oven. Add brandy, if using. Cool.

In a large mixing bowl, beat margarine until fluffy. Add chocolate mixture, beating well. Stir in matzoh and nuts.

Place a piece of wax paper about 2 feet long on a work surface. Use a large spoon to shape a mass about 10" long and 2" in diameter. Wrap the wax paper around it and shape it into a cylinder. Tuck the ends under, place on a plate, and refrigerate at least 3 hours until firm.

Melt glaze ingredients. Unwrap the roll, spoon glaze over it evenly, and chill again. To serve, arrange on platter surrounded by berries. or serve slices on individual plates with a berry or two on the side. Slice with serrated knife. Serves 10-12. (This dessert is very rich, so servings are small.)

Elegant Curried Fruit

A versatile dish that can be served as a dessert if made with crust, or as an accompaniment to entrée, if made without crust. If kosher for Passover curry is not available, make your own. (See page 197)

Matzoh Farfel Pie Crust:

Melt 1/2 pound margarine, mix with 1/2 cup brown sugar.
Mix into 3 cups matzoh farfel to make a pie layer or crust. Press into a 9" pie plate and bake for about 20 minutes at 350^0 F.

> 1 large can of sliced peaches, drained
> 2 small cans of mandarin oranges, drained
> 1 teaspoon curry powder
> Candied fruits (optional)

Drain canned fruit thoroughly. (Reserve fruit juices for later use if desired.) Arrange fruit on farfel crust. Sprinkle curry on top. Dot with candied fruits. Curried fruit pie can be served warm or cold. If served warm, bake matzoh farfel crust for only 15 minutes.   *(Continued)*

Variations: For dessert, omit curry and spread almond cream sauce on top.

For layered cake, make 2 or 3 matzoh farfel crusts. Put peaches on first layer, cover with second crust, put apricots on second layer; cover with third crust. End with crust or with a layer of other fruit.

Note: It is important to drain and dry canned fruits thoroughly, using paper towels, or dessert will be runny and the crust will soften.

Strawberry-Rhubarb Compote

2 cups 3/4" rhubarb slices (10 ounces by weight)
2 medium apples peeled, cored, finely diced
1/3 to 1/2 cup sugar
1/2 to 3/4 cup water
1 quart strawberries, hulled and halved

In a heavy-bottomed 3 quart saucepan, combine rhubarb, apple, 1/3 cup sugar, and enough water to cover. Bring to the boil, lower heat and simmer about 10 minutes, stirring occasionally. When fruit is tender, mash apples and rhubarb into a sauce. Add berries and stir about 5 minutes over low heat. Taste, add sugar as desired. Serve warm or cold, as a compote, or as topping for cake or tofutti. Serves 8 as a compote, more as a topping. For Purim, serve as a sauce for rice.

Prune Treats

A delicious confection for holiday nibbling.

2 pounds prunes, pitted, rinsed and drained
Walnut or pecan halves
1 cup sugar
2 cups sweet kiddush wine

Stuff each prune with a nut half.
Boil sugar and wine until sugar dissolves. Add prunes, simmer gently about 15 minutes. Refrigerate in covered container. Drain before serving. Recipe makes a lot and can be halved. Also a good recipe for Purim and Tu B' Shevat.

YOM HA'ATZMA'UT

Nisan

Menu 1
Stuffed Grape Leaves
Bulgur "Meatballs"
or
Joseph's Coat Salad
Vegetarian Chili
Carrot Salad
Fresh Figs With Anisette

Menu 2
Hummus and Falafel with Pita
Bulgur and Grape Salad
Tofu in Walnut Pomegranate
Sauce With Rice
Date Balls

Recipes for Yom Ha'Atzma'ut At a Glance:
Appetizer: *Stuffed Grape Leaves*
Spread: *Hummus*
Entrées: *Bulgur "Meatballs," Falafel, Tofu In Pomegranate Sauce, Pita Bread Torpedoes, Portobello Mushroom Sandwiches, Slimmer's Chili*
Side Dish: *Syrian-Jewish Wheat Pudding*
Salads: *Barley Salad, Bulgur and Grape Salad, Vegetable Bean Salad*
Desserts: *Fresh Figs with Anisette, Date Balls*

For the Lord has brought us into a good Land,
a land with streams and springs and fountains,
A land of wheat and barley, of vines, figs and pomegranates.
of olive trees and honey (Deut 8: 8-9)

"The experience of first meeting with the soil of Eretz Yisrael at various periods in history received many descriptions in literature. At times, this experience centres on the first contact with the soil of the Holy Land and the first impressions left by its scenery or holy place; at others, it expresses itself in the pleasure of partaking of its fruits and crops."

(Yehuda Feliks, *Nature and Man in the Bible*)

The revered species of Israel are the most ancient foods human beings ate when they began to settle and till the soil, and they were most probably first cultivated in the Middle East or around the Mediterranean basin. In their explanatory notes, the publishers of the sumptuous prints, "Fruits of the Bible, write that:

"The Seven Species represent the entire spectrum of human sustenance of vegetable origin....The Seven Species were brought to Jerusalem on Shavuot, the Holiday of First Fruit Offerings, to express thanksgiving for the bounty with which the tillers of the soil were blessed. A splendid ceremony surrounded the First Fruit Offering, determining the order in which the Seven Species were to be arranged in the ritual basket. The particularly scrupulous would bring each species in its own basket. Jewish tradition ascribes special qualities to the Seven Species. Some say that one who partakes of the Seven Species, will enjoy good health and long life." (Matan Arts, Tel Aviv)

WHEAT

"He makes peace in thy borders and fills thee with the finest of wheat"
(Psalms 147:14)

"You would I feed with richest wheat,
With honey from the rock would I satisfy you."
(Psalm 81)

156

Wheat and barley may have been the first agricultural crops, cultivated as long ago as the seventh millennium BCE. Wheat has been traced to the Neolithic era. More recently, there are references to wheat in Sumerian and Akkadian literature. Waverley Root speculates in *Food,* that "The earliest settlements we know about arose where wheat grew wild; it is probable that they were established there because of the presence of wheat." Today about half of all the cultivated lands in the world are devoted to cereals.

Egypt was the greatest wheat producing country in the biblical era, and wheat became the basis of its economy. Waverley Root writes that the wheat yields in the fertile land around the Nile were as great three thousand years ago as they are today with the best farming technology. Wheat played a major role in the story of Joseph's rise to political importance in the court of the Pharaoh. Root also believes that it was the Egyptians who discovered, probably by accident, the secret of yeast, which weaves its symbolic theme in the Passover story. In its uncooked form, we know wheat best today as bulgur. The following three recipes are courtesy of The Vegetarian Resource Group

Syrian -Jewish Wheat Pudding

    1 1/2 cups bulgur (cracked wheat)
    4 cups water
    1 cup raisins
    1/2 teaspoon caraway seeds, optional
    1 tablespoon pistachio nuts, shelled
    1 tablespoon walnuts, shelled, chopped
    1/4 cup maple syrup

Combine bulgur, water, raisins and caraway seeds in a covered pot. Cook over medium heat 30 minutes. Stir occasionally. Add nuts and syrup. Simmer 5 minutes more. Can be served warm or cold. Serves 8.

Bulgur "Meatballs"

    1 cup bulgur
    3 cups water
    1/2 cup whole wheat flour
    1 carrot, peeled and grated
    3 scallions, finely chopped
    2 tablespoons parsley, finely chopped
    1 teaspoon tamari
    1/2 teaspoon garlic powder
    1 tablespoon oil

157

Soak bulgur in water in a large bowl for 2 hours. Squeeze out excess water with your hands. Mix soaked bulgur with the remaining ingredients, except the oil. Form into 16 balls.

Heat oil in skillet over medium-high heat. Cook bulgur balls in oil, turning every few minutes until brown on all sides. Remove from skillet and place on paper toweling to drain excess oil. Serves 4.

Plan ahead. You can make enough bulgur for this recipe and the preceding one in a single batch.

BARLEY

"Take thou wheat and barley, beans and lentils, millet and spelt, put them into one vessel, and make a bread from them." Ezekiel 4:9

"Health food breads" are not new. Six-grain breads were being baked in biblical times.

Like wheat, barley was cultivated in Neolithic times. Egyptian hieroglyphics dating back 5,000 years ago refer to barley. Because of its low gluten content, it is refractory to the action of yeast and therefore good for unleavened bread. Though its nutritive value is not as good as wheat or rye (though better than rice) it is an excellent grain for desert life. Oded Schwartz notes the following:

" As a rule nomadic people do not ferment their bread as it is difficult to maintain a stable 'sour dough' on the move. Yeast becomes unstable and over-active and eventually dies in the heat of the desert. To the nomad leavened bread was the symbol of permanency, which threatened the essence of the nomadic way of life. In the desert the Hebrews reverted to the food of their origin, the nomadic unleavened bread." (p. 27)

Its significance in Jewish life is apparent in the counting of the Omer, the sheaves of barley, from the second day of Passover to Shavuot, when the Book of Ruth is read. Barley figures in the lovely story of how Ruth met Boaz while gleaning in the barley fields.

Barley also makes an excellent hearty ingredient in cholent. (See recipe for Shabbat)

Barley Salad

3 tablespoons vegetable oil
1 1/2 cups barley
2 1/4 cups cold water
Salt and freshly ground black pepper to taste
1 cup dry roasted, unsalted cashews
1/2 pound small mushrooms
1/2 cup white wine
2 large celery ribs, thinly sliced
1 bunch scallions, thinly sliced
1 cup cherry tomatoes
1 jar (6 ounces) artichoke hearts, drained and halved
1 cup pitted black olives
Chopped fresh parsley for garnish

Vinaigrette:
4 tablespoons oil
2 tablespoons wine vinegar
1 teaspoon mustard
Salt and freshly ground black pepper to taste

For the dressing: combine all ingredients in a small screwtop jar and shake well, or whisk them altogether in a small bowl.

Preheat oven to 350^0 F.
Heat 2 tablespoons oil in a small casserole. Add barley and stir over high heat until grains begin to brown. Add water, salt and pepper. Cover and bake 1 hour, or until liquid is absorbed. The barley should be done but still have some bite. Remove barley to a large bowl. Add enough vinaigrette to moisten. Cool, stirring occasionally.

Cut mushroom stems even with the caps. Heat 1 tablespoon oil in a small skillet. Add mushrooms, salt and pepper. Cook, stirring until brown. Add wine and cook over high heat until wine is absorbed. Cool.

In a large salad bowl, combine barley, mushrooms and all remaining ingredients, except parsley. Stir in enough vinaigrette to moisten well. Taste and correct seasonings. Garnish with parsley and serve at room temperature. Serves 8.

GRAPE VINES

Behold I will allure her and bring her into the wilderness, and speak tenderly with her. And I will give her vineyards from thence, and the valley of Achor as a door of hope; and she shall respond there, as in the days of her youth, and as in the day when she came up out of the land of Egypt. (Hosea ll: 16-17)

The prophets and the Hebrews were keen observers and lovers of the land. Everything that grew in their domain, wheat, barley, the grapevine, the olive tree, found its way into their poetry. Their thoughts about good and evil, sin and judgment were developed through metaphors from nature and the seven species. But the grape vine held a special place. It became the metaphor of God's mercy and God's disappointment. The descriptions evoke sensual delight and disappointment and judgment. Like the vine itself, biblical stories weave the theme of the luscious grapes God found in the desert---which turned sour.

Grapes were probably first cultivated in Persia, and then spread southward. The earliest record of wine--and of drunkenness--is in Genesis, in the story of Noah, to whom the discovery of wine is attributed.

Along with honey and figs, grapes were prized as a source of sweetener for foods. Raisins were made from them by burying them in the sand and letting them dehydrate.

Jews have always been excellent vintners. They cultivated vineyards along the terraced hillsides of Judea in biblical times, and during the early Middle Ages, until about the 12th century, developed vineyards in southern France, in Provence, and in the Crimea.

Bulgur and Grape Salad
(Courtesy of the Vegtarian Resource Goup)

2 cups bulgur
4 cups orange juice
1 pound seedless grapes
(For color, use both dark and green grapes)
2 teaspoons cinnamon

Soak bulgur in juice for at least 4-1/2 hours until juice is absorbed and bulgur is soft. (You can soak mixture overnight.) Cut grapes in half and toss into bulgur. Add cinnamon and stir well. Chill and toss once before serving. Serves 6.

Stuffed Grape Leaves

Always a favorite dish, can be served as hors d'oeuvres or as finger picnic food.

1 cup long grain rice, washed
4 cups chopped onions
1 cup olive oil
2 cups warm water
Juice of 1/2 lemon, or to taste
50 grape leaves
1/2 cup pignoli nuts, browned lightly in oil
2 tablespoons lemon juice
1 teaspoon pepper
2 teaspoons paprika
1/2 teaspoon allspice
2 tablespoons chopped parsley
2 tablespoons chopped dill
1 tablespoon chopped mint
Lemon wedges for garnish

Sauté chopped onions in oil until light brown. Add rice, nuts, spices and herbs. Mix well.

Add 3/4 cup warm water, cover, simmer until water is absorbed.
Cool slightly. Stuff grape leaves.

Place side by side in 2 quart pan and form as many layers as necessary. Add 1 cup warm water and lemon juice. Cover pan with an inverted plate over low heat so that the rolls won't shift.

Cover and simmer over low heat 40-60 minutes.

Can be prepared a day ahead. Serve with lemon wedges. Serves 10-12.

FIGS

Figs probably originated in Western Turkey. They have the highest sugar content of any fruit and were used as a sweetener in ancient times. The honey mentioned among the seven sacred species of Eretz Israel was honey from figs. Assyria made fig syrup, and figs were grown in the hanging gardens of Babylonia. Baskets with figs in them have been found in Egyptian tombs.

Like the grapevine, the fig tree has been immortalized by the prophet Micah (4:4) as an image of peace: "For each shall sit under his vine and beneath his fig tree, and none shall make him afraid."

Fresh Figs with Anisette and Mint Leaves

The Jewish Vegetarian Society in Toronto served this delightful fig dish at the Jewish Vegetarians of North America Conference in 1993.

Wash figs gently in cool water, dry on a clean dish towel. If desired, peel figs. Cut off stems, and cut in half. Arrange on serving plates, 3-4 figs per person. Drizzle with anisette and sprinkle with mint leaves for color and taste.

A dollop of lightly sweetened almond cream or tofu topping can be spooned over figs.

POMEGRANATES

Thou art fair, my love.
Thy temples are like a piece of pomegranate within thy locks.
.....

"...I would cause thee to drink of spice wine, of the juice of my pomegranate."
Song of Songs

And well Solomon should have sung like this, for he kept a grove of pomegranates.

Carbonized pomegranates have been found in a tomb in Jericho, dating from the Bronze Age, and pomegranates were grown in Egypt before the time of Moses. He may have wandered in pomegranate groves. Pomegranate trees were growing in Canaan when the Israelites arrived, and remained a major crop there.

The fruit is believed to have healing and immunizing qualities. Jews revere it as a symbol of fertility, and beautiful men and women are often compared to pomegranates. It is loved for its color, its juice and its shiny seeds.

162

It appears frequently in Jewish mosaics, on coins and building columns, and it is said that the garments of the Temple priests were adorned with pomegranate designs. Many Torah scroll ornaments are in the shape of the pomegranate. Some scholars believe that the "apple" in the Garden of Eden was the pomegranate---which became an apple with Renaissance painters, who were probably influenced by the Greek stories of Helen and the golden apple.

Drinks, juices and sweeteners made from the pomegranate are popular in the Middle East. Grenadine syrup is made from pomegranates, and adds a "sultry" flavor to juices, mixed drinks and cooked fruits.

When buying, choose a fruit that is large to ensure juicy flesh inside. Eat when fruit begins to look dry. Do not keep longer or the skin will harden and be difficult to peel.

Pomegranate seeds make a beautiful garnish for salads.

Tofu in Walnut Pomegranate Sauce

An unusual dish adapted from Ginger Singer's Vegan Cooking Course in Jerusalem

    1 pound firm tofu, cut in 2" cubes
    3 tablespoons oil
    2 medium onions, diced
    1 cup ground walnuts
    1 cup pomegranate juice
    1 teaspoon lemon juice
    2 tablespoons honey
    1 teaspoon ground cardamom
    1/4 teaspoon salt
    Pepper to taste

Heat skillet with 2 tablespoons of oil. Sauté tofu cubes until lightly brown on both sides. Tofu may stick to pan if cooked too long.

In a separate skillet, sauté onions in remaining oil until translucent. Add ground walnuts and sauté another 2-3 minutes. Add pomegranate juice, lemon, honey, cardamom and salt. Mix well and cook about 5 minutes over low heat. Spoon sauce over tofu cubes. Serve over brown rice. Serves 4. *(Continued)*

Note: The sauce may be used as a marinade for tofu cubes. Brown tofu and prepare sauce half an hour in advance before rice is done. Reheat for about 3 minutes. Pomegranate molasses may be used instead of pomegranate juice, but mix with water, equal parts molasses and water, or 2/3 water to 1/3 molasses, depending upon strength of marinade desired.

OLIVES

"My old age shall be like that of the olive, which is forever green."
Targum Jonathan

"An evergreen olive tree, fair with goodly fruit." Jeremiah

"Like an evergreen olive tree in the house of God" Psalm liii:10

Olive trees may first have been developed in Syria about 6,000 years ago. Because of their deep rooting system they are well suited to grow in desert areas and hot countries and found a natural home in the Middle East and the Mediterranean basin. Originally their oil was used for scents, soaps and as a lubricant to keep the body warm, rather than for food. Their wood was considered highly desirable for carving, and Jewish law forbade burning it. Jewish kings were anointed with olive oil and olive wood was used in the tabernacle of Solomon's temple. Olive oil was used as a cleanser and a medicine, for it contains salicylic acid, the active ingredient in aspirin. Olive oil was burned for light. The pulp of the olive was fed to animals and used as a fertilizer. No wonder some historians believe that the olive tree exerted more influence on civilizations than any other fruit tree in its contribution to the economy of the early civilizations of the Middle East and around the Mediterranean.

In Jewish literature, the olive tree is loved for its unusual growing pattern which has come to symbolize endurance, longevity and sometimes immortality. Yehuda Feliks, in *Nature and Man in the Bible,* writes:

"In theory, the olive tree can continue to flourish for an unlimited period. When a tree grows old, its trunk becomes hollow and there is always the danger that fires and winds of unusual velocity may destroy it. The olive tree, however, takes care to ensure its continuity: from its roots around the base of its trunk, it sprouts young shoots. These surround the old trunk and guard it against the destructive winds, and when the hollow trunk finally yields, and the tree breaks, the young shoots take its place....The olive tree more than any other tree, therefore, most suitably symbolizes the righteous [person] whose life is not fleeting like that of the flowers of the field, but, like the olive, bears the hallmarks of constancy and continuity."

In Talmudic times, the rabbis declared that the olive had the same status as wine and could be offered on the altar. (*Talmud Berakhot,* 35A). They also used it as a standard of measurement for other foods. (41B; 47B;48A)

Today, the olive is often demoted to the status of a garnish for salad or a decoration for a martini, but can be used in endless ways in pastas and grains. Always buy good quality olives, green or black. Italian, Greek and near Eastern markets are the best sources. Try different varieties to find those that please your palate.

Large olives can be stuffed with walnuts or with Incredible Spread for an excellent hors d'oeuvre.

DATES

The date palm has the distinction of being the only fruit that is included in both the Seven Species and the four Species of Sukkot. The palm was basic to survival in the desert because of its deep rooting system which allows it to extract moisture from the sand.   The tree has come to symbolize the friend of those who wander in the desert because when it appears, water is close by. It is the "indispensable staple food" of desert people and has been described by Waverley Root as living "'with its feet in the water and its head in the sun,' which makes it the oasis plant par excellence...." The oldest date stones were discovered in Northern Iraq and are 50,000 years old. While these were wild dates, the fruit was cultivated by Neolithic times. Its cultivation requires care, for while date palms are either male or female, the pollen from the female trees is not carried by insects and must be distributed by hand.

The date fruit is extraordinarily durable under desert conditions. It remains tasty, edible and nourishing even when it is dried and will keep for a long time without losing its value. Dates can be kept in the freezer for several months. When defrosted, they taste like new, so don't hesitate to buy good quality dates in bulk.

Date honey was the major sweetener for the Hebrews.

Date Balls

Children will enjoy making and eating these. Older children can do the cooking; younger ones can shape the cookies. Makes about 4 dozen.

> 1/2 cup margarine (1 stick)
> 1 cup chopped dates
> 1 cup sugar
> 2 cups Rice Krispies
> 1 teaspoon vanilla
> 1 cup chopped nuts, optional
> Shredded coconut

In medium saucepan, cook margarine, dates and sugar until dates are soft. Stir in Rice Krispies, vanilla, and optional nuts. Roll into small balls and roll in shredded coconut. Store in covered container in refrigerator.

Falafel

In Israel the holiday is most frequently celebrated with picnics and parties, as is the Fourth of July in the United States.

Falafel is the most famous indigenous food of the Middle East region. You can make your own falafel and experiment with different ingredients, making them as spicy as you like. There are, however, some reliable packaged mixes.

Falafel is a very nourishing food. Made from chickpeas, it is most often served in pita bread with a variety of salads. An interesting way to serve falafel is to have a "falafel bar." Place a platter of falafel on the table, surrounded by a basket of pita bread and plates of chopped salads: lettuce, onions, tomatoes, olives, humus, olive oil and vinegar, and some bottles of hot spices. Let everyone make their own falafel sandwich as they wish.

Chickpeas are a good basis for many recipes, including chickpea fritters and a chickpea loaf which can be made the day before and taken along as picnic food.

Here is one of our favorite recipes for falafel, courtesy of the North American Vegetarian Society, because it is baked instead of fried and is therefore lower in fat.

2 medium potatoes, peeled, cubed and cooked
1 1/2 cups uncooked chickpeas
1 1/2 quarts water
1 teaspoon ground marjoram
2 medium onions, finely chopped
1/2 cup chopped parsley
2 tablespoons oil
2 tablespoons soy sauce
1 teaspoon each of turmeric, cumin,
        garlic powder, chili powder

Soak chickpeas in water overnight. Cook chickpeas in soaking liquid with the ground marjoram for one to 1 1/2 hours, or until tender.

Mash potatoes. Purée chickpeas in processor. Mix potatoes and garbanzos together.

Preheat oven to 350^0 F.
Sauté onions and parsley until onions are translucent and parsley wilts just a bit. Add sautéed vegetables to the potato-chickpea mixture. Add remaining ingredients. Mix well.

Form into small balls and flatten slightly on top. Place on oiled cookie sheet. Bake 10-15 minutes on each side, or until golden brown. Serves 10.

Pita Bread Torpedoes

4 pita breads
Tahini to taste
4 large lettuce leaves
3 roasted, marinated red peppers, seeded, halved
1 large onion, sliced
3 basil leaves
3 tomatoes, sliced thinly

Cut pita bread in half, making two flat disks. Spread with tahini.
Cover each half with layers of lettuce leaf, red peppers, shredded onion, tomato slices, basil leaves. Roll up. Secure with toothpicks. Cut diagonally. Serve with pickles and olives. Serves 4-6.

Hummus

We can remember when it took a day's shopping to assemble all the ingredients for this dish, making it a rare and exotic treat. Now it's as American as Spaghetti-O's, and available at most supermarkets. But homemade is still best! Keep some around to use on sandwiches instead of mayonnaise or other spreads.

2 cups cooked or canned chickpeas, drained
2/3 cup sesame tahini paste
3/4 cup lemon juice (from about 3 lemons)
1 teaspoon salt
1/2 to 1 teaspoon cumin, or to taste, optional
Zhug, optional*
Paprika or cayenne for garnish
Olive oil for garnish, optional
Mediterranean olives, optional
Pita wedges
Assorted medium bell peppers
Mild onions

In a food processor fitted with steel blade, blend chickpeas, tahini, lemon juice, garlic, salt and cumin (if using), until smooth. Taste and correct for lemon juice and salt. Stir in zhug if using. Scrape into shallow serving bowl. Pour a small circle of olive oil in the middle, sprinkle with paprika or cayenne, and dot with olives.

Seed and derib bell peppers and cut them into pieces the length of the pepper and about an inch wide. Cut onions into thick wedges, then take the layers apart to make scoops. Serve peppers, onions and pita wedges with hummus. Serves 8-10.

Note: Zhug is a fiery condiment available in Israel. Bring it back when you visit, if you can't find it locally. Or look for harissa, the Moroccan equivalent in U.S. ethnic markets.

Slimmer's Chili With Vegetables

This chili was created by Gloria Bakst and its fame has spread from mouth to mouth.

 1 large onion, chopped (about 3/4 cup)
 2 cloves garlic, crushed
 1/4 cup dry vermouth or white wine
 2 tablespoons chili powder
 1/4 teaspoon dried basil
 1/4 teaspoon dried oregano
 1/4 teaspoon cumin
 2 cups finely chopped zucchini
 1 cup finely chopped carrot
 1 29 ounce can tomatoes plus 1 14 1/2 ounce
   can tomatoes, drained and chopped
 4 cups cooked kidney beans + one cup of their
   cooking water
 1 tablespoon brown sugar
 1/4 cup soy granules

Garnish: Chopped onions, tomatoes, lettuce and green pepper

In a 4 quart or larger pot, sauté onion and garlic in vermouth or wine until soft. Mix in chili powder, basil, oregano and cumin. Stir in zucchini and carrots. Cook for about 1 minute over low heat, stirring occasionally. Add chopped tomatoes, kidney beans with the 1 cup cooking water, the soy granules and brown sugar. Stir well. Bring to a boil, reduce heat, and simmer for 30-45 minutes or until thick. Top with vegetable garnish. Serves 8-10.

Variation: Can be served over rice or short pasta.

Portobello Mushroom Sandwiches

Portobello mushrooms are expensive, but worth it.

 1/2 pound portobello mushrooms
 2 roasted red peppers, available in jars
 4 dinner rolls
 4 lettuce leaves

(Continued)

Marinade for Mushrooms:
1/4 cup olive oil
2 tablespoons fresh lemon juice
2 cloves garlic, crushed
1/4 teaspoon salt
1/4 teaspoon freshly ground pepper

Marinate mushrooms for 2 hours. Grill mushrooms 3 minutes on each side. Divide mushrooms, red pepper and lettuce into 4 parts and place 1/4 of each inside a roll.

Preparation tip: Portobello mushrooms can be prepared in advance. Can also be served cold in a green salad, rather than in a sandwich.

Vegetable Bean Salad

Another excellent bean dish for picnics, or indoor eating.

1 cup raw long-grain rice, white or brown,
      or 3 cups cooked orzo
15 ounce can kidney beans, drained, rinsed
1 large stalk broccoli, cut up into florets, stems sliced,
      and steamed 5 minutes
1/2 pound snow peas or sugar snap peas
1/2 pound mushrooms, sliced thin

Dressing:
1/4 cup olive oil
2 tablespoons lemon juice
3 tablespoons vinegar
2 large cloves garlic, crushed
1 teaspoon dry mustard
3/4 teaspoon dried tarragon, crumbled
1/2 teaspoon salt, optional
1/2 teaspoon freshly ground pepper

Garnish:
Greens for serving
1 pint cherry tomatoes, halved, optional

In large bowl, combine all salad ingredients.
In a covered jar, shake dressing ingredients thoroughly. Pour dressing over grain and vegetable mixture. Toss salad to mix thoroughly. Refrigerate until serving time.

On a large platter, serve the salad on a bed of greens surrounded by cherry tomato halves. Serves 4 as a main dish.

SHAVUOT

Iyar/Sivan

Shavuot is both an agricultural and a religious holiday. It is also called the "Feast of Weeks," because it occurs at the end of seven weeks after the wave-offering of barley, and seven weeks during which the Omer is counted. The Omer is a sheaf cut in the barley harvest. It was only after the offering of the Omer with proper ritual that the Jews were permitted to eat the grain of the new harvest. Because the holiday (sometimes called "Pentecost" in reference to the five books of the Torah) also celebrates the giving of the Torah to the Jews, it is traditional to eat white foods to symbolize the purity of the Law. The Book of Ruth is read in temples and synagogues to commemorate Ruth's conversion and her receiving of the Torah.

Menu 1
Incredible Spread
and/or Almond Tofu "Cheese" Spread
and Pita Crisps
Cauliflower Crofter's Pie
Carrot Salad With Vinaigrette
White Bean Salad
Tofu "Cheesecake"

Menu 2
White Bean Dip with Crackers
Creamy Cauliflower Soup
Corn Salad
Sautéed Zucchini With Walnuts
Rice Pudding, or
Simple Semolina Pudding

Recipes For Shavuot At A Glance:
Spreads and Dips: Incredible Spread, Almond Tofu "Cheese" Spread, Tofu "Sour Cream," White Bean Dip
Soup: Cream of Cauliflower
Entrées: Cauliflower Crofter's Pie, Joseph's Coat Orzo Salad, Zucchini Sautéed With Walnuts
Salads: Grated Carrots With Vinaigrette, Corn Salad, White Bean Salad
Drinks: Almond Nut Milk, Quick Cashew Nut Milk, Milk Shake
Desserts: Rice Pudding, Simple Semolina Pudding, Tofu "Cheesecake"

Cream of Cauliflower Soup

A beautiful choice for Shavuot.

2 tablespoons extra virgin olive oil
1 large clove garlic, minced
1 jalapeño pepper, cored, seeded, and minced
2 medium onions, diced
1/2 teaspoon ground cardamom
1/8 teaspoon ground mace
1 large cauliflower (about 2 pounds), cored and chopped
4 cups vegetable stock or water
1 cup soy milk
1/4 teaspoon freshly ground white pepper
Minced fresh chives

In 3 quart or larger saucepan or soup pot, heat oil and add garlic, jalapeño, onions, cardamom, and mace. Sauté until onions are translucent and tender, about 5 minutes. Add cauliflower and stock. Bring to a boil, cover and simmer about 30 minutes.

Strain soup into a bowl. In food processor, purée solids. Return purée to pot, add soy milk and stir in enough liquid to make a soup with a creamy consistency. It should not be too thick or too thin. Season with salt and pepper. Reheat carefully over low heat. Garnish with minced chives. May be served hot or chilled. Serves 6.

Cauliflower Crofter's Pie

An unusual combination of tastes

1 tablespoon oil, or spray
6 medium potatoes, peeled and quartered for boiling
1 large, diced onion
2 teaspoons salt, or to taste, divided in half
1 teaspoon cilantro
1/2 teaspoon oregano
1 medium size head of cauliflower florets
1/2 cup minced, sun dried tomatoes
Paprika

Preheat oven to 350⁰ F.

Boil and mash potatoes.

Oil or spray skillet. Sauté onions until translucent. Mix onions into mashed potatoes.

Oil or spray small oven casserole dish (about 7"-8" diameter). Place 2/3 of mashed potatoes on bottom of dish.

Steam cauliflower florets, or cook in 3 " of water until just tender. Mash or lightly purée florets. Add salt and sun dried tomatoes, mix well. Place on top of layer of mashed potatoes. Add final 1/3 of mashed potatoes on top of cauliflower. Brush lightly with oil, or spray lightly. Dust with paprika. Bake uncovered 30 minutes, or until top browns. Serves 6.

Simple Semolina Pudding

Sephardim have many traditional dishes for Shavuot. Prominent among them is the use of semolina, a granular product of durum wheat available in Middle Eastern and Italian markets.

>2 1/2 cups water
>1 cup coarse semolina
>1 cup sugar
>1 cup chopped almonds
>1 teaspoon vanilla extract, or to taste
>1 teaspoon cinnamon, or to taste

In a heavy pot, bring water and sugar to boil. Add semolina.

Reduce heat to lowest level. Continue to stir until water is absorbed and semolina is cooked. Add almonds and vanilla. Pour into a mold and refrigerate. Unmold. Sprinkle with cinnamon. Serve with fruit, or with nut cream.
Serves 8.

Incredible Spread

Umeboshi paste, made from pickled plums and sometimes called ume paste, is expensive, but you only need a small amount for this recipe and it keeps for a long time. It is also suggested in macrobiotic diets as an aid in helping sufferers from migraine headaches.

> 1 pound firm tofu
> 1 tablespoon umeboshi paste
> 1 tablespoon brown rice vinegar
> 1 1/2 tablespoons oil
> 3-4 large scallions chopped fine

In food processor fitted with a steel blade, process or pulse tofu for about 20 seconds until just smooth. Stir in remaining ingredients. Store in refrigerator. Excellent on sandwiches, as a spread, or stuffing for olives, mushrooms, or celery.

Tofu Sour Cream

Courtesy of The North American Vegetarian Society. Can be used as a topping over fruits, or in a sandwich with jams. Combine following ingredients in a food processor and process until smooth and creamy. Makes 2 cups.

> 1/2 cup ground cashews (unsalted is preferable)
> 2 cups tofu cubes (about 3/4 pound)
> 1/8-1/4 cup oil, according to taste
> 1 1/2 teaspoons maple syrup
> 1 tablespoon tamari
> 2 tablespoons lemon juice, or according to taste

Almond Tofu "Cheese" Spread

Shavuot dish created in Ginger Singer's Vegan Cooking Course in Jerusalem.

> 1 cup finely ground almonds
> 1 pound firm tofu, cut in 2" pieces
> 5 teaspoons tamari sauce
> 5-6 cloves garlic, minced
> 2 teaspoons rosemary
> 2 tablespoons red vermouth

Mix all ingredients together in food processor and chill for two hours.

Rice Pudding
(Courtesy of Edensoy)

1 quart Edensoy or any Eden food beverage
1 3" stick cinnamon
1/2 teaspoon cardamom seeds, crushed
3 whole cloves
3/4 cup cooked white basmati rice
2 tablespoons any nut butter
2 tablespoons maple syrup

Combine Edensoy, cinnamon, cardamom seeds and cloves in a saucepan, and bring to a boil. Add rice. Turn down heat to low and simmer, covered, 60 minutes. Discard cinnamon stick and cloves. Stir in nut butter and maple syrup. Serve warm or chilled. Serves 5-6.

Joseph's Coat Orzo Salad

The many colors of this salad recall that most famous of biblical garments, though its wearer almost certainly never tasted pasta. Orzo cooks quickly, making it a good choice for warm weather menus.

1 1/2 cups orzo
1/4-1/3 cup olive oil
3 tablespoons lemon juice
1/2 teaspoon grated lemon zest
1/2 teaspoon salt
1/8 teaspoon freshly ground black pepper
1 garlic clove, crushed
1 medium carrot, shredded
1 1/4 cups total finely diced red,
      green and/or yellow bell pepper
1/2 cup peeled, seeded, finely diced cucumber
1/4 cup finely chopped scallions
1/4 cup finely chopped red onion
1/4 cup finely chopped basil or dill

Cook orzo until tender, according to package directions. Drain well, rinse under cold water. In a small bowl or screwtop jar, combine oil, lemon juice, lemon zest, salt, pepper and garlic. In a large bowl, mix the orzo, vegetables, herb, and dressing. May be served warm or at room temperature. Serves 4-6. Can be doubled.

Zucchini Sauté With Walnuts

Just the dish for a houseful of holiday guests. The zucchini can be kept at room temperature for an hour or two. Rewarm briefly.

> 1/4 cup oil
> 2 tablespoons chopped onion
> 8 cups thinly sliced zucchini (about 6 medium)
> 1/2 cup chopped walnuts
> Salt and pepper

Warm oil in large skillet over medium heat. Add onion and sauté until translucent; add zucchini. Cover and cook 15 minutes or until tender, stirring occasionally. Add walnuts just before serving. Season with salt and pepper to taste. Serves 6-8.

Grated Carrots With Vinaigrette

It is difficult to determine portion sizes for this salad. Its unusual, nutty dressing gives it a richness rare in the realm of salads. So, while a small portion, half a cup, should suffice, this salad is so good that people may well want more. To forestall the Jewish cook's nightmare of running out of anything during a holiday, we are offering larger-than-usual servings.

> 6 cups coarsely grated carrots (about 2 pounds)

> **Dressing:**
> 3 tablespoons walnut oil
> 1 1/2 tablespoons vegetable oil
> 3 tablespoons wine vinegar
> 1 1/2 teaspoons Dijon mustard
> 1 teaspoon salt, or to taste
> 3 or 4 grinds freshly ground black pepper

In a small saucepan, combine dressing ingredients. Just before serving, heat them, and mix gently but thoroughly with carrots in a large serving bowl. Serves 8.

Corn Salad

A small amount of work yields a large amount of brightly colored, intensely flavored salad.

2 20-ounce packages of frozen corn kernels,
    cooked according to package directions, and drained
1 cup chopped scallions, green and white parts
2/3 cup chopped pimentos
1/4 cup red wine vinegar
2 tablespoons Dijon mustard
1 tablespoon honey
1 teaspoon minced garlic
1/2 teaspoon dried thyme
1/2 teaspoon ground cumin
1 teaspoon salt
1/2 cup olive oil
Freshly ground pepper to taste
1/2 cup chopped cilantro or parsley

Mix the corn, scallions and pimentos in a large bowl.

In a small bowl, beat together the vinegar, mustard, honey, garlic, thyme, cumin, salt and pepper. Add oil in a slow stream, beating steadily. Dress the salad. Add the fresh herb and toss gently until thoroughly mixed. Use a slotted spoon to remove the salad to a serving bowl. Serves 8.

White Bean Salad

White beans make a variety of dishes that are good for Shavuot. The following can be served warm as is, or served chilled on a bed of greenleaf lettuce.

2 cups of cooked small white beans
        (1 cup of uncooked beans)
2 tablespoons olive oil or generous spray
1 medium onion, minced
1 medium green pepper, seeded and diced
2 ripe tomatoes, in coarse chunks
Pinch of chili pepper
Salt and black pepper to taste

178

Oil or spray skillet. Sauté onion until translucent. Add green pepper. Cook for about 5 minutes. Add tomatoes. Cook another five minutes. Add cooked white beans and seasonings. Cook over low heat another five minutes, or until most of the liquid is absorbed. If chilling, cool first, then remove to bowl and refrigerate. Serves 6.

White Bean Dip

There are many versions of bean dips. This one is based on Ginger Singer's recipe from her Vegan Cooking Course in Jerusalem.

3 cups cooked white beans
1/2 cup bean liquid, reserved from cooking
1 teaspoon minced garlic
3/4 cup tahini
1/4 cup + 1 tablespoon lemon juice
5 teaspoons tamari
Minced parsley, optional

Purée beans in food processor with 1/2 cup of bean liquid. Add remaining ingredients, pulsing slightly after each addition. Serve on bread or crackers, or as a dip with vegetables.

Note: If you prefer a firmer spread, omit or reduce the bean liquid.

Almond Nut Milk

4 cups water
1 pound blanched almonds
1 cup sugar
1/4 cup orange blossom water

Divide ingredients into four batches to be pulverized in blender or food processor in equal amounts: 1 cup of water, 1/2 cup almonds, 1/4 cup sugar, 1 tablespoon orange blossom water. Press each mixture through a cheesecloth and blend again. Repeat process until the 4 batches have been used up. If desired, dilute mixture with water or crushed ice cube.

Quick Cashew Nut Milk

Suggested by The Vegetarian Resource Group.

1 cup raw cashews
3 cups water

Blend ingredients together for five minutes and refrigerate. Shake before using. Makes about 4 cups.

Tofu " Cheesecake"

Adapted from Muriel Golde's recipe for the North American Vegetarian Society.

Pie crust of your choice, or graham cracker crust. (page 62)

Preheat oven to 350^0 F.

Filling:
2 pounds tofu, cut up
1/4 cup lemon juice
1/4 cup mild flavored oil
1 cup maple syrup
2 teaspoons vanilla
1 tablespoon arrowroot powder

Combine filling ingredients in blender and process until creamy. You may want to do this in two batches. Pour into pie plate. Bake 40-45 minutes, until top is golden brown and filling has jelled. Makes a 9" pie.

Tip: Garnish with thin lemon slices, standing up like wheels.

"Milk" Shake

3 cups nut milk from one of the above recipes
Cocoa and Sweetener to taste
2/3 cup shredded coconut (optional)

Blend ingredients together at high speed for 2 minutes. Serve chilled. Makes 3 cups.

Life Cycle Menus

From ancient times, round foods have been regarded as symbols of the cycle of life and have been traditional in menus for brit milah, bar mitzvah, weddings and funerals. Today, we not only serve them at the traditional ceremonies for Jewish boys, we also include them in the simchat bat (baby-naming ceremony for girls) and bat mitzvah menus. At the vegan table, challah, bagels, and round legumes like chickpeas and lentils, appear in this role. (Plain boiled, salted chickpeas, "nahit," are an easy and popular way to serve chickpeas.)

To design a buffet menu for a crowd, choose from the following selection of breads, dips, finger foods, fork foods and desserts. Always have wine for kiddush. If you don't like the sweet kiddush wine, consult a knowledgeable wine merchant for alternatives.

Usually, the larger the crowd the more dishes you will want to have. Most recipes can be doubled easily. If you serve tofu pie, you will need to bake more than one if you serve more than 10 people.

Skewers of seasonal fresh fruit are a nice addition to any party menu. Consult index for the following recipes.

Buffet Selections

Breads:
Challah, bagels, pita
Molasses-Orange Bread

Finger Foods
Stuffed Grape Leaves
Kishke
Knishes (should be served hot)
<u>Serve the following with appropriate Breads</u>:
Spinach Dip, Incredible Spread, Walnut Paté, Hummus

Fork Food
Lentils and Rice with Caramelized Onions
(can be served at room temperature or hot)

Desserts

Several of the following cakes are very rich. If you serve more than one cake, serve one rich cake and one that is less rich.

Chocolate Tofu Pie
or
Chocolate Cake
or
Baklava
Applesauce Cake

Skewers of Seasonal Fresh Fruit
With An Assortment of the Following Cookies:

Snowball Cookies
Chocolate Pecan Cookies
Date Balls
Chocolate Peanut Butter Squares

For A Sit-Down Buffet

The following menus are delicious, eye-appealing and easy to manage.

Appetizer:
Stuffed Mushrooms--Hot

Two or three of the following Entrées
Spicy Peanut Sesame Noodles
Lentils and Rice with Caramelized Onions
Uppuma
Rotini and Vegetable Bake
Any Chili With Rice
Spiced Chickpeas with Rice
Joseph's Coat Orzo Salad

Two or three salads
Quinoa Salad
Barley Salad
Potato Salad
Corn Salad

Fattoush Salad
Israeli Salad
Marinated Cucumber Salad
Spinach-Apricot Salad
Any Carrot Salad
Cabbage, Apple, and Nut Salad

Vegetables:
Marinated Cucumbers
Green Beans Provencale
Broccoli Vinaigrette

Sample Menu for a Sit-Down Buffet I:

Knishes
Spinach Dip with Pita
Mock Chopped Liver with Pita
Spiced Chickpeas and Rice
Corn Salad
Marinated Cucumber Salad
Cabbage, Apple and Nut Salad
Chocolate Tofu Pie

Sample Sit-Down Buffet Menu II:

Stuffed Grape Leaves
Walnut Pâté With Pita
Nahit
Rotini Vegetable Bake
Carrot Salad With Ginger
Quinoa Salad
Israeli Salad
Applesauce Cake
Cookie Platter

Sample Sit-Down Buffet Menu III

Incredible Spread with Bagels or Pita
Hummus and Pita
Kishke
Lentils and Rice With Caramelized Onions
Broccoli Vinaigrette
Joseph's Coat Orzo Salad
Fattoush
Poached Pears
Snowball Cookies

Defining Vegetarian, Vegan, Pareve

Vegan foods may often be the same as pareve foods, but not always. They may overlap, but they are not synonymous. It is possible for a processed vegan food which has no animal products in it to have been prepared in pots that contained animal products so that it is not pareve. On the other hand, some products could be pareve, but not acceptable to a vegan. For instance, marshmallows made from gelatin produced from animal bones which may not have been ritually slaughtered, can be considered pareve, because the bones have been so altered in the manufacturing process that the definition of kosher no longer applies to them. Animal products find their way into many other unlikely products, such as cosmetics, soaps, textiles, and paint brushes. Blood, which is proscribed for Jews, can be found in many products. A list of these can be obtained from the Jewish Vegetarians of North America or The Vegetarian Resource Group.

Labels on all products should be checked. The concerned vegan, who may not have previously thought about the pareve label, would benefit from knowing the label. The kosher pareve label certifies not only that the food contains no meat or dairy products, but that it has not come in contact with meat or dairy products in the manufacturing process.

Natural, unprocessed, unmanufactured foods of no animal origin are the best guarantee that the food is kosher. For the careful vegetarian Jew, the best food to eat is both vegan and pareve. The following is a partial list of manufacturers of pareve/vegetarian foods. They do not constitute an endorsement, and labels should be checked, because the definitions of "kosher" and "pareve" are fluid in this age where foods undergo complex transformations. As vegetarian and vegan foods become more mainstream, there will be more manufacturers of kosher vegan foods which you can add to this list. The fact that there are quite a number available already indicates the growing interest of Jews in vegetarian and vegan foods, and the growing interest of non-Jewish vegetarians in the kosher/pareve label as a guarantee of their interests. For a more extensive list and discussion send a self addressed, stamped business envelope and $1.00 to The Jewish Vegetarians of North America and request their newsletter, The Jewish Vegetarian Newsletter, Volume XlII, no. 1, Spring 1996.

The American Miso Co., Rt. 3, Box 541, Rutherford, NC 28139 (704-287-2940)

Arrowhead Mills, 110 South Lawton, Hereford, TX 79045 (806-364-0730)

Eden Foods, 701 Tecumseh Rd., Clinton, MI 49236 (517-456-7424)

Fantastic Foods, 106 Galli Dr., Novato, CA 94949 (415-883-7718)

Hain Pure Food, 400 S. Fourth St., St. Louis, MO 63102 (314-622-6541)

Jaclyn's Food Products, P.O. Box 1314, Cherry Hill, NJ 08034 (609-938-2560)

Joyva Corp., 53 Varick Ave., Brooklyn, NY 11237 (718-497-0170)

Kashi Co., P.O. Box 8557, La Jolla, CA 92038 (619-454-6186)

Lightlife Foods, P.O. Box 870, Greenfield, MA 01302 (413-772-0991)

Nasoya Foods, 23 Jytek Dr., Leominster, MA 01453 (508-537-0713)

Pacific Rice Products, 460 Harter Ave., Woodland, CA 95659 (916-662-5056)

Spectrum Marketing, 133 Copeland St., Petaluma, CA 94952 (707-778-8900)

Stow Mills, P.O. Box 301, Stow Dr., Chesterfield, NH 03443 (603-256-3000)

Tomsun Foods, Int'l., 247 Wells St., Greenfield, MA 01301 (413-774-6501)

Twenty-First Century Foods, 30A Germania St. Jamaica Plain, MA 02130 (617-522-7579)

U.S. Mills, 395 Elliot St., Newton Upper Falls, MA 02164 (617-969-5400)

White Wave, 1990 N. 57th Ct., Boulder, Co. 80301 (303-443-3470)

For recipes in this cookbook, the following sources are especially useful: Arrowhead, Casbah, Erewhon, Eden, Hain's Eggless Mayonnaise, Nasoya Nayonaise and Tofu.

Conversion Table

A brief list of equivalent measures, rounded off for ease in cooking

U.S.	Metric
1 ounce	28 grams dry weight, or 29.5 milliliters by volume
1 pound	454 grams
1 teaspoon	5 milliliters
1 tablespoon	15 milliliters
1 cup	.240 liter
1 pint	.470 liter
1 quart	.950 liter
1 stick margarine	.100 grams
1 inch	2.5 centimeters

Tips About Tofu

Tofu is a great mixer and can accompany many dishes. It is an inexpensive form of protein, which can be used in a variety of recipes, such as tofu loaves, tofu burgers, sloppy joes, stir fries, sweet and sour dishes with green peppers and pineapples. It can be fried, baked, and marinated. One of the virtues of tofu is that it marinates quickly, within 30-60 minutes. Almost any marinade will do, even simple tamari or soy sauce.

Tofu is extraordinarily adaptable and versatile. It can be used in main courses, or to make dips, spreads, dessert creams, and cakes. Soy foods broaden the kosher taste experience. Kosher soy products now include pareve ice creams like Tofutti, soy cheeses, and soy meat analogs for foods like bacon and fish.

With all these virtues, it is also healthy. Eating soy beans may decrease the risk of colon and rectal cancer, and perhaps even breast cancer because they contain isoflavin, which seems to prevent estrogen from binding to human cells and forming tumors.

However, by itself tofu has little taste, so don't make the mistake of buying a package of tofu and eating it as is. (It isn't harmful to eat it that way, it just isn't tasty.)

You can buy 1 pound or 10 ounce blocks of tofu in many supermarkets. (Always check the expiration date as you would for any food). Tofu is packaged in liquid to keep it moist and fresh. To use, slit the package open and drain well. Place in a colander for about 10 minutes, then pat dry with kitchen towelling. Or place a heavy dish over the block of tofu in the colander and press down to squeeze out moisture.

Tofu blocks are available in "firm," "extra firm," "regular," "soft" or "silken" textures. Recipes generally specify which type you will need. Firm and extra firm are the most useful; they contain the least water and hold their shape best in cooking.

Once the package of tofu is opened, it is best to use it up or freeze it. It can be stored in water for about three days in the refrigerator in a closed container, in water to cover. The water should be changed daily. Drained and wrapped well in plastic wrap, it will keep in the freezer for many weeks. To defrost at room temperature takes about six hours, so if you use frozen tofu plan accordingly. After defrosting, squeeze out remaining moisture with kitchen toweling. Frozen tofu marinates well and adds heft to dishes like chili.

An excellent introduction to the versatility of tofu is *Tofu Cookery,* by Louise Hagler (Book Publishing Company, Summertown, TN 38483).

Tofu's cousin, tempeh, is a cultured food, like yogurt. It is made of a mixture of cooked soybeans and grains, or of soybeans alone, bound together by a harmless mold. (Spots on the surface are a result of this mold.) Tempeh is sold frozen or refrigerated. Like tofu, it can be marinated, cubed, sliced, fried, oven fried, used in sandwiches with onions, sauerkraut or ketchup. It makes for a fast, easy sandwich, high in complete protein and if not fried, low in fat. Always keep refrigerated or frozen.

About Grains

Beans and whole grains were the foundation of diets in the past, until about a century ago.   Each region had its prized grain from which hundreds of foods were made. Rice was the grain of the Asian world; wheat and barley of the Middle Eastern world; corn was the basic grain for the North and South American Indian; quinoa was the prized grain for the Incas, and sorghum and millet the grains of Africa. Today, we can enjoy the blessings of all these grains. They are making a deserved comeback as nutritionists discover their inestimable contribution to health, and as modern cooks create more and more delicious dishes for them. For a history and discussion of grains, a useful book is *Grains for Better Health,* by Maureen B. Keene and Daniella Chace.

It is best to eat whole grains, rather than processed grains. Rinse thoroughly before cooking. Grains and beans can be cooked easily in modern pressure cookers. Consult Lorna Sass' books, *Complete Vegetarian Kitchen* (originally published as *The Ecological Kitchen)* or *Cooking Under Pressure.*

Wild rice cooked with long or medium grain rice adds a nice texture; also adding a few wheat berries to rice gives it a crunchy texture. If blending rices and/or grains, cook according to directions for the dominant grain.

Brown basmati rice is a bit more expensive than standard brown rices, but particularly flavorful, and has a wonderful aroma. It should be cooked according to directions for brown rice.

It is economical to buy rices and grains in bulk, but don't stock up on more than you can use in two or three months. Store in a tightly closed canister or jar on a cool, dark shelf. You can freeze grains for five to six months. They can also be stored in the refrigerator for 4 months. Reheat leftover cooked grains in a rice steamer or the top of a double boiler.

The following is a timetable for commonly used grains, but explore others and add them to the list. In general, the rule of thumb in cooking grains is 2 parts water to 1 part grain, first bring water to a boil, add grain, then cook covered over very low heat for about half an hour (one hour for brown rices). Check tables for specific details. Do not stir while grain is cooking. Count on about 1 cup of cooked grain per person. Grains benefit from standing 5 to 10 minutes after being cooked, so factor standing time into your cooking of grains.

Barley expands a great deal, 1 cup dry to 3 or 4 cups cooked and requires 3 parts water to one part grain, and 40 to 45 minutes cooking time. Pearl barley has had its husk and almost all its bran removed. It is advisable to buy pearl barley in health food stores, since they often carry a pearl barley which has a layer of bran to protect the germ. Hulled barley has only the outer husk removed and the texture is chewier.

Grain	ratio of water to grain	cooking time	yield
barley (pearl)	3 to 1	40-45 minutes	3 cups
barley (hulled)	3 to 1	1 1/2 hours	3 cups
buckwheat groats (kasha)	2 to 1	25 minutes	2 1/2 cups
bulgur	2 to 1	25 minutes	2 1/2 cups
couscous	2 to 1	15 minutes	3 cups
quinoa	2 to 1	15 minutes	4 cups
brown rice, long, or medium grain	2 1/2 to 1	50 minutes	3 cups
short grain	2 to 1	40 minutes	3 cups
white rice	2 to 1	25 minutes	2 cups
wild rice	2 1/2 to 1	40 minutes	3 cups

About Dried Beans and Other Legumes

Most beans benefit from an overnight pre-soaking, except for lentils and peas. Presoaking can reduce the time needed for cooking by several hours, and some people claim that it cuts down on the reaction of gassiness. However, gas is often a temporary problem, as the digestive system usually adjusts to eating beans. There are also several products on the market, such as "Beano," which might help eliminate gas. If you have a problem, look for a solution without eliminating beans from your diet. They are too healthy to forego.

Store beans on a cool, dark, dry shelf, preferably in a glass jar with a tight cover. Beans can be kept for six months; however, they tend to harden and dry as they age and this can lengthen cooking time.

Drain off the soaking water and cook beans in clean, fresh water, about double the volume of beans. Bring water to a boil, lower heat to simmer, and cook with the pot lid slightly ajar. Most beans swell to 2 1/2 times their dry volume, so cook in a large enough pot. Test one or two beans to see when they are done. Taste or roll them between two fingers. They should be soft, but not mushy. Test for doneness about 1/2 hour before end of allotted cooking time. Do not add salt to beans until they are finished cooking.

If you cook more beans than you need, drain and freeze the remainder without water in a tight fitting container. Frozen beans can be kept for 3 months, and you will be a step ahead when you make your next bean dish. You can use as needed for spreads or in soups, or any bean dish. If cooked beans are stored in the refrigerator, however, use within three days.

The following is a list of commonly used beans, but there is now a profusion of "boutique beans," such as calypsos, black valentines, scarlet runners, tongues of fire, rattlesnake, Steuben yellow eye. If you are intrigued by these, consult *Lorna Sass' Complete Vegetarian Cooking* (p. 171-177), and add them or others to this list for your record.

Always rinse beans thoroughly in a colander even if they are organic, because dust can settle on them. Cooking time is given in the first column for pre-soaked beans, except where pre-soaking is not necessary, and in the last column for unsoaked beans.

Bean	Presoaked	Unsoaked
Chickpeas (garbanzos)	2 hours	3-4 hours
Fava Beans	1 1/2-2 hours	2-3 hours
Lentils	no soaking	45 minutes
Lima beans	about 50 minutes	1 1/2-1 3/4 hours
Split peas	no soaking	about 50 minutes
Whole peas	no soaking	1 to 1 1/2 hours
Pinto Beans	1 1/2 to 2 hours	2-3 hours
Red Kidney Beans	1 1/2 to 2 hours	2-3 hours
Beige Soybeans	2 to 3 hours	3-4 hours
White Beans or Great Northern Beans	1 to 1 1/2 hours	about 2 hours

Note: Instead of soaking overnight, you can bring the beans to a boil, and let sit for an hour before cooking.

Cooking Without Eggs

The following suggestions are from *Instead of Chicken, Instead of Poultry,* by Karen Davis.

It is easy to forego eggs when you remember that they contain about 70% fat, and an average egg contains 250 milligrams of cholesterol, and may be contaminated by salmonella bacteria. Generally, if a recipe calls for only one egg, it can be omitted.

To hold foods together in casseroles, burgers and loaves:

For white sauces made with soy milk or nondairy cream, use mashed potato. Amounts will have to be adjusted to specific recipes.

To leaven, bind, and liquefy in baking. Each of the following is for one egg.

1 tablespoon arrowroot powder + 1 tablespoon soy flour + 2 tablespoons water (if needed).

2 tablespoons flour + 1/2 tablespoon vegetable shortening + 1/2 teaspoon baking powder + 2 tablespoons water.

2-4 tablespoons tofu, blended with liquid called for in recipe.

2 tablespoons cornstarch or potato starch.

2 tablespoons arrowroot flour.

1 heaping tablespoon soy powder + 2 tablespoons water.

1/2 to 1 banana, mashed.

1 tablespoon flax seeds + 1/4 cup water. Blend flax seeds and water in blender for 1-2 minutes, till mixture is thick and has the consistency of unbeaten egg white.

Oils and Vinegars

Recipes in this cookbook call for olive oil, sesame oil, vegetable oil, or safflower oil, and hot Chinese oil (usually as an option).

Vegetable oils are usually canola, safflower, corn, or a mixture of these. Occasionally, a recipe may call for walnut oil. Opinion is often divided about their nutritional and taste merits, and the decision is personal. Vegetable oils are not quite as healthy as olive oil, but lighter in taste, and many people prefer to sauté in a vegetable oil.

Whether sautéing in vegetable or olive oil, if you are calorie or fat conscious, try "sweating" your vegetables. Put a thin layer of oil in the skillet or pot, just enough to cover the bottom, heat a little, then place your vegetables in the pot, mix well to coat vegetables lightly with the oil. Cover skillet. After about 2-3 minutes, add more water as needed to continue cooking the vegetables. Add more water as water evaporates, to prevent the vegetables from burning. This method partly sautés and partly steams the vegetables. The vegetables will taste as if they have been sautéed.

The method works well with onions, green beans, green and red peppers, brussel sprouts. With green beans, peppers and brussel sprouts, cover vegetables after water has been added and cook for five to ten minutes, depending on how tender or chewy you want the vegetable to be.

Olive oil has the greatest nutritional virtues, for it is high in monounsaturated fats, but it can be heavy in taste and it is also often more expensive than vegetable oils. Olive oil aficionados feel about olive oil as wine aficionados feel about wines. Labels of "Extra Virgin, "Virgin, and "Cold Pressed" can be confusing. "Extra Virgin" indicates that the oil was made from the first pressing of the olive and therefore has the fullest flavor. "Cold pressed" means that the oil has not been refined. "Virgin" refers to the second pressing. Olive oil should be stored in a dark bottle. It can be kept for as long as eighteen months, perhaps two years, if it is not exposed to sunlight. Olive oil is expensive, because gathering the olives is a tedious, time-consuming job, as all the olives in an orchard, even on the same tree, do not ripen at the same time. Some caution should be practised in purchasing olive oil. Because a good quality is expensive, it is sometimes tempting to buy a poor quality oil, but you must be sure you know what this oil has been mixed with. In 1981, thousands of Spaniards became sick when olive oil from France was mixed with improperly processed rapeseed oil.

Chinese hot oil and sesame oil are condiments. Sesame oil has an exotic flavor. A few drops added to other oils for stir-fries, or sprinkled over grated carrots transforms a simple dish. It is often used in Oriental cookery. Hot Chinese oil is not for the faint-hearted, and should be used sparingly, when you want to give sauces a "punch."

The variety of vinegars available is astonishing, and each one can impart a distinctive flavor to your salad or marinade. There is apple vinegar, wine vinegar, white balsamic vinegar, red balsamic vinegar, tarragon vinegar, rice vinegar, brown rice vinegar, apple sage vinegar and herbal vinegars.

The quality and price of these vinegars varies a great deal; experiment to find out what you like. Rice vinegar is nicely mild, but if too mild, add a few drops of wine vinegar to it. You can mix mild vinegars with a few drops of a more acerbic vinegar to satisfy your taste.

Herbs, Seeds, and Green Things

See, I give you every herb, seed, and green thing to you for food.
(Gen. 1:28-30)

Two centuries ago, herbal gardens were often still attached to medical schools and doctors were required to know the uses of herbs. All societies practised herbal medicine before the modern era. But here we are concerned only with herbs as food. Like grains and legumes, herbs are making a sensational comeback, adding luster and zest to our meals. They are the great temptresses of the taste buds. A few basil or sage leaves or some dill will transform your soup or salad. But as with vinegars you must make the choice of what to use and how much. The only requirement with herbs is that they be as fresh as possible.

If you have a little land, even a plot of two feet by two feet, you can plant two or three herbs. They require less care than vegetables and will grow in window boxes, on terraces in a city, even in a pot in a sunny window. In the midst of winter, you can pluck a basil leaf from a pot on your windowsill and make a salad taste like the outdoors. If it is possible, plant a herb or two in pots or boxes, because they have become expensive to buy.

Herbs and spices can change the nationality of a dish. Vegetables become Italian vegetables when cooked with garlic and oregano or basil; they become Mexican when cooked with cumin or red pepper; they become Indian when cooked with curry and ginger. You can sprinkle them on baked potatoes, on bread, on rice, on celery ribs, on sliced tomatoes. You can put them in soups and on salads, and vary their taste each time you use a different herb.

Many of our favorite flavorings, like coriander, mustard, dill, aniseeds, caraway, fennel, nutmeg, and poppy come from the seeds of plants. Seeds in general have been valued for their health for centuries. Seeds, which are not herbs, like sunflower seeds and sesame seeds are also healthy, high in protein, but also high in fat. These may be sprinkled on foods and in salads, lightly roasted or plain.

The following is a list of commonly used herbs and suggestions for their use. It is difficult to describe tastes, unless they are distinctively bitter or sweet, so each cook must make the voyage of discovery. Notice which herbs are useful for fruits, desserts, in baking, in salads or in soups, and which herbs pair together or work well together so that each brings out the other's flavor.

Aniseed imparts a licorice flavor to foods, and is interesting to use on fruit desserts. Try it sparingly at first.

Basil is the beloved herb in pasta and Italian dishes, but is equally good in soups, salads and grain dishes of any nationality.

Bay leaves are used mainly in soups and stews, and should be removed before serving the dish.

Cardamom comes in tiny hard seeds, and can be bought whole or ground. Try it on sliced bananas, baked apples, or sweet potato pudding.

Caraway is most often used in rye bread, but is welcome in cole slaws, potato salads, and noodle dishes.

Cayenne pepper is used in hot spice mixtures, curries, chutneys and chilis.

Chives are a sweeter form of onion or scallion. Nice in soups or chopped into salads. They are an extremely easy-to-grow perennial.

Cilantro is a green herb long used in North African and Mexican cooking, now newly popular everywhere.

Cinnamon is possibly the most popular spice used in baking. It combines well with nutmeg and/or sugar for toppings on puddings and baked fruits.

Cloves are also popular in baking and on stewed apples and sweet potato puddings, but try them in vegetable stews and chilis for a surprising flavor. They are available whole or round. Remove whole cloves before serving.

Coriander is the seed of the cilantro plant, good in soups, bean dishes, curries, and chilis.

Cumin is excellent for Mexican, Indian, and Middle Eastern dishes. Many cooks like to mix coriander and cumin together.

Curry can be bought ready-made. Curries vary in quality and you should decide which kind appeals to you, or make your own from a mixture of two teaspoons each of ground coriander, cumin, and turmeric; 1 teaspoon of ground nutmeg, 1/2 teaspoon of salt, 1/4 teaspoon cayenne pepper and freshly ground black pepper, to taste.

Dill is a favorite herb for salads and soups, and in pickling.

Fennel also has a licorice flavor, but not as strong as anise. It is used in salads, baking and on fruit desserts.

Garlic, popular in most of the world, is the darling of Italian and stir fry recipes. Its medicinal value has adherents and opponents. It is related to the onion family and can be sautéed together with onions. (See Helpful Hint # 6)

Ginger, like curry, is good in Oriental dishes, vegetable stir fries, and on baked fruit dishes. Use sparingly, since its flavor is usually strong.

Marjoram is similar to oregano, but milder, and used in similar Italian-style dishes and in other cuisines.

Mustard comes in many forms, ground dry, as seeds, and wet. The seeds can be used to combine with curries, ginger and cumin. When using in stir fry vegetables, sauté 1 tablespoon quickly in hot oil until they begin to pop.

Nutmeg combines well with cinnamon, and is good for cooked fruit desserts. Try it sparingly on cooked, puréed broccoli or spinach for a surprising flavor.

Oregano is often called the pizza herb. It is associated in use and taste with marjoram, but is stronger.

Paprika, the sweet Hungarian type, is useful on stewing onions for flavor and color. There is also hot paprika, which should be used cautiously.

Parsley is often used--and wasted--as a garnish. It is wonderful in salads and soups, and for making pesto.

Poppy is used to make mohn for filling hamantashen, but can be used all year round in noodle dishes.

Rosemary is most often used in tomato-based dishes, but try it in breads, muffins, and simple cakes for a different flavor. It can also be used sparingly in salads and soups.

Sage has a strong flavor, usually recommended for soups, but try it cut up finely on salads. Use sparingly.

Tarragon is used most often in salads, and in vinegars.

Thyme is a dainty herb, used in Italian and French recipes, and in tomato stews. Sprinkle it on grains and in bean dishes.

Turmeric gives food a rich yellow color. It is most often used along with ginger and curries.

Green Things, or Salads

A mixed green salad is always welcome. Use a variety of lettuces and greens to make your tossed salad different and more interesting. Try romaine, green leaf, oakleaf, arugula, spinach, dandelion greens, kale and mustard greens in any combination.

Drying greens in a salad spinner just before mealtime can be a nuisance. If you have time, wash them in the morning. Spin them in a salad spinner for about a minute, then let them drain in a colander during the day, in the refrigerator if you have the room; if not, on a counter top. Before using, pat with kitchen toweling, if necessary, to remove any remaining moisture. Salads should be made as close to meal time as possible.

Use fresh produce for your salad, organic if possible.

Good olive oil with a mild, light rice vinegar or freshly squeezed lemon is a classic salad dressing. Spoon the oil over the greens, using just enough oil to coat the vegetables, and toss well. (You should not have a puddle of oil at the bottom of your salad bowl.) Add the spices, salt, crushed or minced fresh garlic or garlic powder, and herbs, and toss thoroughly. Add the vinegar or lemon juice last and toss one more time.

If you wish to prepare the salad dressing in advance, first dissolve salt, garlic powder and dry mustard in vinegar in a small bowl or screw top jar, add oil, and stir or shake well. You can make your own distinctive salad dressings, by mixing olive oil with your desired vinegar, and adding your favorite herbs and a pinch of salt. The amounts will depend on how much salad dressing you want. In general, the ratio is 3/4 cup of olive oil to 1/4 cup vinegar, but the amount of vinegar depends on whether you are using a mild or sharp vinegar. Diet-conscious cooks can reduce the proportions to 2-1.

To the oil/vinegar mixture add 2-4 tablespoons or more of herbs, again keeping in mind that the amount of herbs used depends upon which herbs you use, whether mild or pungent, and what kind of taste you like. Use the freshest herbs available. The dressing can be made ahead without the fresh herbs, which can be added later as dressing is used, with different herbs chosen to go with different meals. (Herbs can turn brown and lose their fresh appearance if left standing.) If not using herbs and/or fresh garlic, the dressing need not be refrigerated. With fresh garlic, it must be. Shake well, and refrigerate for two weeks. With a little experimenting, you can make your own gourmet vinegars and dressings. Put up in nice bottles, they make wonderful gifts. The following salad dressings suggest some possibilities.

Lime-Cumin Dressing

This dressing from The North American Vegetarian Society is so rich in flavor it should be used sparingly.

> 1/4 cup olive oil
> 2 tablespoons lime juice
> 1/2 teaspoon maple syrup
> 1/2 teaspoon ground cumin
> 1 teaspoon tamari sauce
> 1 clove garlic, minced

Place all ingredients in a small jar with a screw lid. Shake vigorously before serving. Can be refrigerated for a few days. Yields about 1/3 cup.

Lemon-Herb Dressing

A variation on Lime-Cumin Dressing. Replace lime juice with lemon juice, and the cumin with a teaspoon of dried thyme--or 1/2 teaspoon of dried tarragon.

To vary your basic salad, toss in leftover cooked, chilled vegetables. The vegetables that work best for this are green beans, cut in 2" lengths, sweet red pepper cut in 1" chunks, 1/2 cup of cold green peas, or 1/2 cup corn niblets. These vegetables can be served mixed together on a leaf of lettuce, or tossed into the salad in any combination. Leftover grains and beans can also be tossed into a salad. The following are other salad suggestions:

Fiddleheads and Mushrooms Salad

Fiddleheads are available only for a few weeks at the beginning of spring. They are expensive, but so light that 1/4 pound is usually enough for a salad for 4-6. Some people feel that their delicate flavor comes through best when they are sweated or lightly sautéed and served with freshly squeezed lemon juice and a pinch of garlic powder. Others prefer the following recipe.

> 2 tablespoons olive oil
> 2 cups of fiddleheads
> 2 cups of mushrooms, sliced

Sauté fiddleheads briefly in 1 tablespoon of oil. Set aside.
Sauté mushrooms in 1 tablespoon of oil until just limp.

Mix fiddleheads and mushrooms together. Chill for one hour. Can be tossed with greens and favorite dressing.

Kale Salad

Sauté a pound of kale until just limp. (It will shrink in cooking.) Sprinkle with fresh lemon juice and 1/2 teaspoon garlic powder, or to taste. Chill for about an hour. The kale can be tossed in with a green salad or eaten as is.

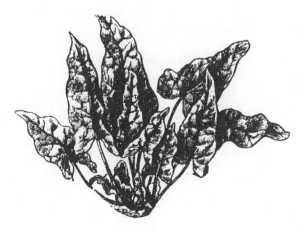

Useful Addresses

The International Jewish Vegetarian and Natural Health Society, 8 Finchley Road, London NW11 8LX., UK. Publishes a quarterly and are affiliated with the International Vegetarian Union; supports a Children's Home in Israel, at Rehov Brazil 14, P.O.B. 9722, Jerusalem. Jerusalem Office is at 8 Balfour Street, Jerusalem, Israel. Offices in Australia are at: Level 1, 387/9 Glenhuntly Road, P.O. Box 693, Elsternwick, Victoria 3185; and 6/3 Ocean St., Bondi, NSW 2026.

Jewish Vegetarians of North America, 6938 Reliance Road, Federalsburg, MD 21632, is affiliated with The International Jewish Vegetarian and Natural Health Society, and publishes a newsletter, *The Jewish Vegetarian.* For a copy of recent newsletter, send $1.00 with a stamped, self addressed, business envelope.

Jews For Animal Rights, 255 Humphrey Street, Marblehead, MA 01945, is affiliated with The International Jewish Vegetarian and Natural Health Society, and Jewish Vegetarians of North America. Through Micah Publications, they publish books, booklets, and ritual material on Jewish vegetarianism such as vegetarian haggadot, as well as material on Judaism and animal rights, educational material for bar/bat mitzvah and confirmation students, and support a speaker's bureau.

The Vegetarian Resource Group, P.O.B. 1463, Baltimore, MD 21203, publishes a magazine on health, ecology and ethics, *Vegetarian Journal,* which includes recipes and articles of interest for Jewish vegetarians.

The Jewish Vegetarians of Toronto is an active group. For information, write to Evelyn Dorfman, 113 Balliol St., Toronto, Canada M45 1CZ.

The North American Vegetarian Society (NAVS), publishes a newsletter and conducts Vegetarian Summerfest, a weeklong conference every summer; has hosted The World Vegetarian Congress and The International Vegetarian Union. For information, write to: Box 72, Dolgeville, NY 13329.

American Vegan Society conducts the bookstore for vegetarian conferences, and has an extensive listing of vegetarian and vegan titles. For information, write to P.O. Box H, 501 Old Harding Highway, Malaga, NJ 08328.

Selected Bibliography

There are many interesting and provocative books on the history of food in general, and of vegetarianism specifically, as well as many excellent vegetarian cookbooks. Some have been mentioned in context. The following books are cited for their relevance to arguments that have been put forth in this cookbook.

General Jewish Background:

John Cooper, *Eat and Be Satisfied: A Social History of Jewish Food* (Jason Aronson, 1993).

Oded Schwartz, *In Search of Plenty: A History of Jewish Food* (England, 1992).

Jewish Folklore and Ethnology Review, vol. 9, no., 1, 1987 (YIVO Institute for Jewish Research), 1987. Good issue for reviews of books on Jewish food.

On Kashrut:

Samuel H. Dresner, *The Jewish Dietary Laws (*Burning Bush Press, 1966). Revised and Expanded by The Rabbinical Assembly of America, 1982.

Rabbi Yacov Lipschutz, *Kashrut: A Comprehensive Background and Reference Guide to the Principles of Kashrut* (Mesorah publications, Ltd., 1995).

Joe M. Regenstein, "The Kosher Food Market in the 1990s--A Legal View," *Food Technology,* October, 1992.

Kashrus Magazine, November, 1994 (New York). Contains extensive list of kashrut labels.

Jewish Vegetarian Books:

Louis Berman, *Vegetarianism and The Jewish Tradition,* (KTAV, 1982).

Roberta Kalechofsky, *Vegetarian Judaism----A Guide for Everyone* (Micah Publications, 1998)

Roberta Kalechofsky, ed., *Rabbis and Vegetarianism: An Evolving Tradition,* (Micah Publications, Inc., 1995).

Haggadah For The Liberated Lamb: For a Vegetarian Seder (Micah Publications, Inc., 1988).

Haggadah For the Vegetarian Family (Micah Publications, Inc., 1993).

Israel Sprouts: Guide to Vegetarian Eating in Israel (Vegetarian Resource Group, 1996)

Other Relevant General Books

Ruth Harrison, *Animal Machines* (London, 1964). One of the first books to expose factory farming. Important foreword by Rachel Carson.

Roberta Kalechofsky, ed., *Judaism and Animal Rights: Classical and Contemporary Responses* (Micah Publications, Inc.,1992). Section on shechitah and the relationship of vegetarianism to Judaism.

Jim Mason and Peter Singer, *Animal Factories* (Harmony Books, 1990). Description of how meat animals are raised for today's market.

Jeremy Rifkin, *Beyond Beef: The Rise and Fall of the Cattle Culture* (Dutton, 1992). Good general over-view of the history of beef.

John Robbins, *Diet For A New America* (Stillpoint, 1987). Discusses environmental and health damages related to meat diet.

Steven Rosen, *Food For the Spirit: Vegetarianism and the World Religions* (Bala Books, 1987). Preface by Isaac Bashevis Singer.

Orville Schell, *Modern Meat* (Random House, 1984). Exposition of the uses of antibiotics and chemicals in meat foods.

Elijah Judah Schochet, *Animal Life in Jewish Tradition: Attitudes and Relationships* (Ktav, 1984). Important discussion on the biblical sacrifices and eating of meat.

Index